**BISHOP DR. VANESSA BENSON**

*A Gift :*
*for the good -*
*May God bless the*
*Work of Jour hands*

# THE SECRET PLACE

30/04/2022

Bishop Dr. Vanessa Benson

This book was printed in the United Kingdom

## THE SECRET PLACE

Copyright © 2020 by Bishop Dr. Vanessa

All rights reserved.

Unless otherwise marked, all scriptures quotations are taken from the Holy Bible (NIV) version.

A catalogue record for this book is available from the British library

Distributed by:


Launchers Evangelistic Ministries
International (L.E.M.I)


Website: www.lemi.org.uk


Edited & Published by:


Launchers Evangelistic Ministries
International (LEMI)


Cover Design by: Bluwave Limited

CONTENTS:

## DEDICATION

I dedicate this book to God the Father, the Son and the Holy Spirit who has empowered and given me strength, enabling me to compose it, believing that you will be blessed. This is because the church must be in unity which is the epitome of bringing it together with one goal.

I also dedicate it to my grandchildren who have brought joy into my heart especially when I hears them call me **"CUCU"** **(Grandma)**. I hope when they come to age, they will be exceedingly inspired, together with those who are yet to come. Also, to all my spiritual children all over, may the Almighty God bless you all, protect you, give you peace, prosperity and stability in Yeshua's Mighty Name.

**BY THE MERCIES OF GOD THIS BOOK HAS BEEN TRANSCRIBED!**

## ACKNOWLEGEMENT

I acknowledge God Almighty for giving me courage, strength and determination to remain committed in this enterprise. To my son Moses Collins Mwangi, his wife Dionne, and my grandsons Noah and Eli Mwangi. May the Lord bless and protect you all in Yeshua's Mighty Name. Thank you for your love, support and sacrifice. Your generation will celebrate you.

To my family and friends through association, I celebrates you and may God honour you in Yeshua's Name. I also acknowledges my Spiritual father, his Eminence Archbishop J. Paul Hackman, for his unfailing love, He is my God given Father, my Apostle, my councillor, my reassurance, and my mentor, together with his wife.

Special thanks to all Members of my Ministry Launchers Evangelistic Ministries International (LEMI) all over the world. You are amazing children and may the Lord lift up your head, may you rejoice for your cup will over flow in Yeshua's Mighty name.

## CHAPTER ONE

## THE TRUE PLACE OF SAFETY

This book will strength my readers and show them on how to trust on God entirely in all aspects of life and its stages. This will only be by trust and focus on God who is the author and finisher of our faith. However, the Psalmist tells us this: "Whoever dwells in the shelter of the Most High will rest in the shadow of the Almighty **Psalms 91:1**. This is to say that God will protect and deliver us from all pestilence.

Only when we know to stay in the holy of holies. Before our Saviour Jesus paid the price, it was only the high priests who were allowed to go to the Holy of Holies. We should therefore have an inner sanctuary (secret place) where we guard our heart with all diligence. This is a place of piece with no contamination of anything. Avoid bringing your hurts pains and your disappointments in your inner sanctuary.

Be consistence with the peace of God that surpasses all understanding. It's for sure we have feelings but even though it's a reality protect your inner place.

Sometimes, things may go very wrong like when we lose those we love and dear to us. Your children may go wayward but control your door ways and give notice of dislodgment to all harmful reports, worries and the like. Paul said none of all these, troubles me for there may be a shipwreck and it may be destroyed but he had an assurance none of the people will perish. He had learnt to stay in secret place. What is "the secret place of the Most High"? This is a place of safety an "inner chamber, the place within where we consciously meet God. A hidden place unrevealed and inaccessible to any outside person.

It is the secret place of the Most High that Jesus refers to when He says, "Believe me that I am in the Father and the Father is in me." In **John**. **14:11**, Jesus also affirms the truth of an innermost spiritual sanctuary when he said the kingdom of God is in the midst or you in **Luke 17:21**.

Paul adds Christ in you, the hope of glory in **Colossians 1:27**. People everywhere are seeking refuge from outside forces perceived as negative and dangerous.

Moreover, for us to possess an inner place of safety it is very crucial that we have peace of mind, and avoid relying on anything material, rest we get disappointed. No one can protect us except hiding in the secret place of the Most High God. In this uneasy and superficial world of materiality wealth, fame is all seldom offer for there is constant change since even the markets are fluctuating, bank account dissolved, heath is deteriorating and evaporation of corporate powers, our hope is God only.

We need to know that once we enter our secret place of the Most High, eternal protection awaits us. We enter a realm of assurance, calmness, serenity, and peace. This divine intersection of God, Christ, and our highest consciousness provides a pinnacle of silent power. In this secret place open only to us, we rest in this superb perfection of our spiritual heritage.

We become infused with the essence of God. In this essence lies not only security but a relief from all outer conditions known or unknown to us.

Therefore, we enjoy the enrichment that comes from alignment with Spirit, so that we can then experience love, wisdom, peace, joy, life, and all the positive attributes that come from the reflection of God realized. This place of inner peace becomes our ultimate sanctuary. Blessed by the presence of God, it serves as the grand provider of every spiritual and material need. We are comforted, encouraged, and strengthened. Challenges of health, prosperity, and disharmony in the world may come even in our private kingdom of the Spirit, but we find the solace and energy to confront, embrace, and overcome any negative appearance in God only.

If we take Job as an example for the first thirty chapters, he kept silent allowing people to speak. The bible says in **Job 32:8** "But it is the spirit in a person, the breath of the Almighty, that gives them understanding."

Remember the real you are your spirit, so it's important to dwell in the secret of your creation.  Job was waiting for inspiration and it must have been very uncomfortable to wait for thirty chapters but he waited. He was stretched and had difficulties but waited.  God want us to wait until his time arises for you will surely know when it's time.  There could be tension of endurance but wait for the bible has promised us in **Isaiah 46:4** "Even to your old age and grey hairs I am he; I am he who will sustain you.  I have made you and I will carry you; I will sustain you and I will rescue you."

Also, we are encouraged by the scriptures when David said, I waited patiently for the LORD; And He inclined to me and heard my cry.  He brought me up out of the pit of destruction, out of the miry clay, And He set my feet upon a rock making my footsteps firm. He put a new song in my mouth, a song of praise to our God; Many will see and fear, and will trust in the LORD **Psalms 40:1-3**.  Learn to remain in the **secret place** and the Lord will perfect that which concerns you.  Also, the bibles say, for those who are evil will be destroyed, but those who hope in the LORD will inherit the land **Psalms 37:9**. We may not even know them because sins of the spirit such as hatred, bitterness, being malicious we cannot see, for what we see in the outside cannot tell what is in the inside but we have the judge our father in heaven.

Many go to church but that does not make them Christians. Someone said even if you sleep in a garage you cannot wake up being a car. Take care of your attitude so it does not corrupt all what life has to offer you. Just remain in your **secret place** and you will not go wrong. Remain in the undisclosed place my reader and be a matured person and avoid acting what you are not and evade very minor things to make you lose important opportunity for lack of flesh control. Make quality decision for its stronger than emotions.

When you have your mind changed you become like the prodigal son who came to his senses and chose to change his way of thinking **Psalms 62:5-6**; Yes, my soul, find rest in God; my hope comes from him.

Truly he is my rock and my salvation; he is my fortress; I will not be shaken. Remember to be like an eagle that really understands what it means to wait. When it is waiting it knows for sure it will mount up one of the coming days. We have the wings of the Holy Spirit and we can be elevated by them if we learnt to wait in our **secret place**.

The Scriptures have made us to know that, the eyes of all look to you, and you give them their food at the proper time **Psalms 145:15**. The **Secret Place** is like living that time all over again, plummeting from childhood to adulthood, emerging to a world tremendously distorted yet identifiable, but feeling misunderstood by every person around and desperate to satisfy them all.

The bible says in **1 Corinthian 10:33,** even as I try to please everyone in every way. For I am not seeking my own good but the good of many, so that they may be saved. All you need to know is, you are a child of God and make your ways pleasing to God.

I have sacrificed my life to preach the gospel. The measure of welfare is the one that energies us to keep moving forward to the direction he want us to go. All we need is to have one mind, one passion and one zeal to move forward even as we number our days and apply wisdom in day to day activities. Never lose the zeal and sense of direction, lest you lose the larger sense of God's purpose over your life.

## CHAPTER TWO

## WAITING IN THE SECRET PLACE

Elihu waited, and said the Spirit of the Lord Almighty has given him inspiration and was about to fly. He rebuked Job for saying he was without sin for God is greater than any mortal in **Job 33 vs 12**. Likewise, he said, he was like a new wine skin ready to burst. Learn to be silence before God for He is listening to you even when all looks ugly. For they that wait upon the Lord they shall mount up with wings as an eagle. He listened to the three friends talking to Job.

Therefore, these three men stopped answering Job, because he was righteous in his own eyes. Consequently, Elihu son of Barakel the Buzite said: I am young in years, and you are old; that is why I was fearful, not daring to tell you what I know. I thought, 'Age should speak; advanced years should teach wisdom.' But it is the spirit in a person, the breath of the Almighty, that gives them understanding. It is not only the old who are wise, not only the aged who understand what is right.

Therefore, I say: Listen to me; I too will tell you what I know. I waited while you spoke, I listened to your reasoning; while you were searching for words, I gave you my full attention. But not one of you has proved Job wrong; none of you has answered his arguments. Do not say, we have found wisdom; let God, not a man, refute him. But Job has not marshalled his words against me, and I will not answer him with your arguments. They are dismayed and have no more to say; words have failed them as recorded in the book of **Job 32:6-15**.

When you by pass the flesh you are no more human and you can fly far than mount Everest which is 29,000 feet high. An eagle has four times the accuracy of a man's sight which means, its sharp and so quick and intelligent, it has insight to decern. It is alert, very vigilant and watchful, it has perception and so sensitive. It has awareness and so always awake, with keenness for enthusiasm.

An eagle has passion and willingness and zeal when it has to capture its prey.

It can carry a 7-8 times heavier prey and fly high. Jesus asked his disciples for how long shall I stay with you? Since the church has refused to wait, one demon can take the whole clan to cast out. How can you handle heavier weight if you are not flying high brethren? You will consult and consult but it will not work. Stay in your **secret place** before you can fly and then confront the devil.

Remember when Elijah confronted the king and said Except by my word there will be no rain for three and a half years. He went back again to him and told him now prepare yourself for I hear the abundance of rain. Elijah gave Ahab advance knowledge and if you have God's advanced knowledge you will run. This can only happen in your **secret place** of waiting.

You will walk in confidence until people will ask are you also among the prophets like they asked about Saul. If you wait you will receive inspiration and you can run and then walk. According to **Isaiah 40 :31** the bible says, but those who hope in the LORD will renew their strength.

They will soar on wings like eagles; they will run and not grow weary; they will walk and not be faint.

The bible says in the book of **John 12:35,** Then Jesus told them, you are going to have the light just a little while longer.  Walk while you have the light, before darkness overtakes you.  Whoever walks in the dark does not know where they are going.  He was encouraging them for a time was coming when they cannot do anything to stop what was about to happen.

The scripture also says in **Galatian 5:16-17** So, I say, walk by the Spirit, and you will not gratify the desires of the flesh. For the flesh desires what is contrary to the Spirit, and the Spirit what is contrary to the flesh.  They are in conflict with each other, so that you are not to do whatever you want. We should therefore avoid limiting ourselves.

It is the enemy's scheme to use our challenges in life to keep us doubting, weary and ultimately settling for less than what God has planned for us.

God is a God of no limits.  This year and hence fourth there will be no limits in our speed, travel, money and every area of our life.  We need divine order to receive that which God has planned for us.  He did it for Job and so He can do it for us for He is the same yesterday, today and forever **Psalms 105:37**.

The faithfulness of God to His people is guaranteed if only we avoid having clouded mind for it would not differentiate the messages from God.  Be still and hear the Lord for He has made His prophets the custodian of His priesthood along with the saving doctrines and ordinances of the gospel of Jesus Christ.

As we wait for the second coming of our Lord and Saviour the soon coming King, let's be careful of our thoughts because it can bring us down and can affect our progress. We ought to should exercise our opportunity, power and breakthrough in our **secret place** of waiting.   **Matthew 11:15** "He, who has ears to hear, let him hear."

We shall subdue nations and gates shall not be shut; kings will be stripped their armour for us in Jesus name. Our families, our marriages, our finances shall never terminate prematurely in Jesus name, for the earth is the Lords and its fulness. The bible says in **Philippians 4:13** "we can do all things through Christ who strengthens us."

I declare and decree that no member of our family shall be feeble, no death, no lamentation for I decree good health and none shall die or be eliminated in Yeshua's Mighty name. Our loved ones are coming out of the spirit of complacency and none shall be sick, none shall be destroyed but shall be strong in as we wait and intercede in our secret places so that the son of man can be made manifest.

Having therefore obtained help of God to this very day, I continue unto this day, stand here and testify to small and great alike. I am saying nothing beyond what the prophets and Moses said would happen, "That Christ should suffer, and that he should be the first that should rise from the dead, and should show light unto the people, and to the Gentiles according to the book of **Acts 26:22-23**. This was an offensive message to all the hearers. Paul was risking and so we take risk and glorify God even to them who do not want to hear about our Lord and saviour Jesus Christ (Yeshua Hamashiach).

We could have gone through crisis like Job and it could even have been complicated, but we never made it today by ourselves but God in His mercy he helped us. We will not die in our closet but we are coming out from where we are and we will show up like an eagle in our season, just like Job waited patiently and, in the end, he was restored.

I broke the jaws of the wicked and snatched the prey from his teeth. Then I thought, I shall die in my nest, and I shall multiply my days as the sand. My root is spread out to the waters, and dew lies all night on my branch **Job 29:17-19**. We probably never thought what we have gone through so far would change, but God is helping us to be stirred and our situations will change permanently for there will be no

Limits.  Steel gates will give way in our place and once again kings will be striped for us in Jesus name.

We never knew who to trust, or talk to, but we are coming out and follow Christ who is the author and finisher of our faith.  He has renewed our strength so we could keep watch.  Sometimes we speak to people seeking for counsel but they leave us worse than they met us.  Job got it from friends and even from his wife but thank God who had given him the power and will to wait on Him.

It is our responsibility to believe God and come out of our comfort zones and follow God as that season of discomfort and limitations is over. Our real experience with God will stir us up and help us to derive out of our small corner and soar up as an eagle.  **Matthew 8:20, and Luke 9:58** say, when he called his disciples Jesus said to them, the foxes have holes and birds have nest, but the son of man has nowhere to lay his head.  Think again about a King of kings not having a place to lay His head.  Why?  He was on mission which had to be accomplished in whatever form or shape.

From now saints, we will fly towards the sun as an eagle for the son of man has redeemed us to an extent that our enemy cannot cope and so cannot continue to pursue us as long as before we took off, we had waited in our **secret place**. He will make our feet to run like a deer as the bible says so in the book of **Habakkuk 3:19**. The Sovereign LORD is my strength; he makes my feet like the feet of a deer; he enables me to tread on the heights. God will also make us strong like the sons of Issachar in the book of chronicles who were very strong men and their feet was like of a donkey.

In **Philippians 3:13-14** the bible says, Brethren, I count not myself to have apprehended: but this one thing I do, forgetting those things which are behind, and reaching forth unto those things which are before, I press toward the mark for the prize of the high calling of God in Christ Jesus. My readers avoid dwelling on the past, you are a saint. Come out of your failures and know God is a good God and He cares for us.

Yes, we know, Moses killed an Egyptian man, but God used him to lead the Children of Israel. David committed adultery, yet he was a man after God's own heart and God used him to write most of the Psalms. Paul persecuted the church and killed Christians before he was saved. Whatever our failures were in the past, though great be our fall, God's mercy and pardon are offered to all of us. consequently, in **Romans 10:17** the bible says, faith comes from hearing the message, and by hearing the word of God.

## CHAPTER THREE

## HOLDING ONTO

It is very important to hold onto the promises of God. The scriptures have made us to know that, the righteous will flourish like a palm tree, they will grow like a cedar of Lebanon; planted in the house of the LORD, they will flourish in the courts of our God. They will still bear fruit in old age; they will stay fresh and green **(Psalm 92:12-14)**. Joseph had an incredible story we can all emulate. What is it that you have gone through and has a truck record in your time? So, Pharaoh asked his officials, "Can we find anyone else like this man so obviously filled with the spirit of God?"

Joseph was put in prison because he was falsely accused of rape. The Lord turned his negative to positive. He was being prepared to get into the office of a prime Ministers. Make a difference between clean and unclean. In the dungeon he got his training. In the darkest of the prison the light penetrated and produced a picture that all loved to look at. His brothers came after they were hit by famine and the

Lord used Joseph to radiate the light to them and he blessed them.

That which they made negative became positive for them as it were for Joseph. All our negative experience, to be thrown into pit, sold to slavery, hated by our own, sickness, luck etc. the Lord has turned them to positive for His glory. By grace of God you have survived storms, threats, fear, sickness, witchcraft, accidents and death. If it had not been for the Lord who was on our side, when our enemies rose up against us then they would have swallowed us alive.

Then Pharaoh said to Joseph, "Since God has revealed the meaning of the dreams to you, clearly no one else is as intelligent or wise as you are. You will be in charge of my court, and all my people will take orders from you. Only I, sitting on my throne, will have a rank higher than yours." Pharaoh said to Joseph, "I hereby put you in charge of the entire land of Egypt."

At that moment, Pharaoh removed his signet ring from his hand and placed it on Joseph's finger. He dressed him in fine linen clothing and hung a gold chain around his neck. Then he had Joseph ride in the chariot reserved for his second in command. And wherever Joseph went, the command was shouted, "Kneel down!" So, Pharaoh put Joseph in charge of all Egypt. And Pharaoh said to him, "I am Pharaoh, but no one will lift a hand or foot in the entire land of Egypt without your approval." **Genesis 41:38-44**.

Joseph would have made a choice to revenge when he saw his brothers who had sold him as a slave. Nevertheless, he chose to operate in a place of peace instead of dwelling on the pain. He closed his place of intimacy. He guarded his **secret place** and this is to say when we are faced with trouble such as rejection, hatred and the like in all these times learn to go to your secret place and hold unto God. Remember offence and hatred will not allow you to protect your inner sanctuary. May we guard our hearts as **proverbs 4:23** says, above everything else guard your heart, because from it, flow the springs of life.

Mary the mother of Jesus had to hold on to what she was promised by the angel when he visited her. She must have gone through rejection and hatred and she must have heard a lot of negative talks within the domain she was in. One of the secret things she knew was that she had not known no man yet, she was expecting a baby. She knew she was to be misunderstood but she put up with all rumours and negative talks making sure that she protects her inner sanctuary not to be polluted. If we avoid dwelling in what we hear and concentrate with the promises of God, then we will be settled in our secret place. We will be at peace with God who is able to make beauty out of ashes. I encourage you my reader to let go so you don't miss God's best for you.

However, the colleague could be rumour mongering behind you trying to tarnish your name, avoid allowing gossip to get you distracted. Guard your secret place as you hold un to the one who has promised you rest. Do not be insecure because the devil is using media and haters of progress because the devil is a deceiver, just avoid all negative chatters and do not allow the poison to get in you.

This can only be achieved by one who is holding on in a secret place with closed door. I pray that God will help you to pretend everyone loves you so that you can continue to be hopeful and positive with the things God has promised you.

If you guard yourself then God will take care of your enemies and he will clothe them with shame publicly as he vindicates the one, He loves. Never live an illogical life, just allow God to make you beautiful by letting Him arise and scatter your enemies in many directions, only if you hold on in the secret place. A prophet of God Elijah had to set himself apart waiting for God to equip him for the next assignment. He had to wait in the brook for a period of three and half years.

It was in his holding unto in the secret place that God gave him another assignment to go and meet the widow of Zarephath. In **1 Kings 17:7-16** the word of God affirms that, sometime later the brook dried up because there had been no rain in the land.

Then the word of the LORD came to him: Go at once to Zarephath in the region of Sidon and stay there. I have directed a widow there to supply you with food. So, he went to Zarephath. When he came to the town gate, a widow was there gathering sticks. He called to her and asked, "Would you bring me a little water in a jar so I may have a drink? as she was going to get it, he called, "And bring me, please, a piece of bread."

The Scriptures has made us to know in the book of **Genesis 29**. The younger of twins, Jacob was born holding on to his Brother Esau's heel. His name means "he grasps the heel" or "he deceives." Jacob lived up to his name. He and his mother Rebekah cheated Esau out of his birth right and blessing. Later in Jacob's life, God renamed him Israel, which means "he struggles with God." Jacob was one of the great patriarchs of the Old Testament, but at times he was also a schemer, liar, and manipulator.

God established his covenant with Jacob's grandfather, Abraham. The blessings continued through Jacob's father, Isaac, then to Jacob and his descendants. Jacob's sons became leaders of the 12 tribes of Israel. Then Jacob said to Laban, "Give me my wife that I may go in to her, for my time is completed." So, Laban gathered together all the people of the place and made a feast. But in the evening, he took his daughter Leah and brought her to Jacob, and he went in to her.

Laban gave his female servant Zilpah to his daughter Leah to be her servant. And in the morning, behold, it was Leah! And Jacob said to Laban, "What is this you have done to me? Did I not serve with you for Rachel? Why then have you deceived me?" Laban said, "It is not so done in our country, to give the younger before the firstborn. Complete the week of this one, and I will give you the other also in return for serving me another seven years." Jacob did so, and completed her week. Then Laban gave him his daughter Rachel to be his wife.

Laban gave his female servant Bilhah to his daughter Rachel to be her servant. So, Jacob went in to Rachel also, and he loved Rachel more than Leah, and that is why he served Laban for another seven years. On his fourteenth year the Lord developed his negative into photograph.  It was no longer in darkness but light had comprehended it **Genesis 29:21-30**.  I would like to say to you my reader that reformation will help us to take transformation as we reorganise ourselves making room in our **secret place**, which is our inner place of intimacy.

As you read this book this is the time of your unlimited favour, unlimited breakthrough, a year of making wise decisions in Jesus name.  Jacob served for fourteen years and he got that which he worked for.  May we receive that which we have laboured for this year in Yeshua's Name.  In fact, Jacob struggled with God his entire life, as many of us do.  As he matured in faith, Jacob depended on God more and more.  But the turning point for Jacob came after a dramatic, all-night wrestling match with God.  In the end the Lord touched Jacob's hip and he was a broken man, but also a new man.  From that day forward, Jacob was called Israel for God changed his name.

And for the rest of his life he walked with a limp, demonstrating his dependence on the Lord.

Jacob finally learned to give up control to God. Jacob's story teaches us how an imperfect person can be greatly blessed by God not because of who he or she is, but because of who God is. May we desire to mature in God, this time around like Jacob without compromising our faith in Yeshua's Mighty Name. When we learn to wait on God, He will envelope us and keep us protected in our inner chambers, our sanctuary. This is where we get equipped and we should maximise as we get aligned with God.

Build your personal relationship with God in your holy of holies because this is where salvation is released and revival that we are all talking about will be birthed. Since God want intimacy with those who are seeking Him, we close ourselves in to avoid distraction as we are praying to the father who is also in His secret place. He is already in our waiting place just like the widow who was asked by the prophet what do you have? She said only a little oil and the prophet told her go borrow vessels and close the door and pour the oil that you will have enough to sell and to use.

It is only in closed doors even in the natural we have intimacy with our husbands, and so close the door to have an intimacy with God. It is in the secret place God will announce you that you are his war club and his weapon for battle according to **Jeremiah 51:20**. Our Lord Jesus was the ultimate will of God but he had to pray all night. This made his disciples to desire to know how to pray and they asked him Master, teach us how to pray.

We should never allow our material possessions to hinder us from having intimacy with God. Ester had intimacy with God when she made the whole Nation to fast and pray. When she went to see the king the story that Haman had planned was overturned because she held on to the promises of God in her secret place. Let's not be like Martha the sister of Jesus friend Lazarus. She was busy trying to attend the visitors until she complained that her sister was not helping. Jesus told her Mary has chosen to spend time with her master and so let's desire to be like her.

In the book of **Acts 28:1-6** Paul after the sheep wreck shocks a viper into the fire. People thought he was a god that he was not dropping while others thought he was witch. As you read this book, shake the viper off your hands and crush his head in Yeshua's Name. God is turning our negativity to positivity in His Mighty Name. Let's not forget the dark places of the earth are full of the habitations of cruelty **Psalms 74:20** but we must fortify ourselves with the conviction of our faith especially in this contemporary society. Yes, I mentioned earlier Paul said I have finished my cause.

If you have determined to seek God in your **secret place** then your destiny is guaranteed because we have God and cause of life. You should therefore finish your race and finish it well. We should know that destiny is a magnet that draws us to where we are going and we must remain focused to the cause. Be careful not to fail to recognise your season so you do not detriment yourself. Avoid stagnation, keep walking the walk. Do not go around the mountain for long it's good to know the time to advance when it comes.

Your mind must change for nothing has power like a changed mind so that the same experience doesn't keep on disseminating over and over in the circle of our life.

Follow peace with all men for without it you cannot see God. Stop wasting your energy on negative issues and avoid blaming people around you for your failure. Change your mind. The sun and the moon have a wonderful relationship. The moon is not a light but it reflects light that it gets from the sun. Yeshua is the Sun of righteousness Malachi **4:2** and the bible says we are the Children of light. Therefore, all our negatives must produce positive because light has taken over and darkness must give way to light in Yeshua's Name.

Stay in your **secret place** my reader and wait on the Lord. May your enemies and haters of progress be destroyed in Yeshua's Name, for I demand no peace to the wicked for the Lord will not allow your foot to stumble. The word of God is a lamp unto my feet and a light unto my path by which I see and apprehend the greater levels of glory.

Make this scripture your prayer point "I am the true vine, and my Father is the gardener. He cuts off every branch in me that bears no fruit, while every branch that does bear fruit, he prunes so that it will be even more fruitful **John15:1-2**. There is need to have a connection with God just like Jesus Christ is with the father. Our hope and living only comes from God, and this should be our layout connection with God. May I emphasize the need to have connection with God and you will be real and strong. You can only be strengthened through prayer and be connected to His dimensions.

God spoke to Moses in **Exodus 24:12** which says, The LORD said to Moses, "Come up to me on the mountain and stay here, and I will give you the tablets of stone with the law and commandments I have written for their instruction." The scripture continues to say that for forty days and forty nights he stayed on the mountain. The Lord spoke to him after six days and gave him instruction.

God loves your presence in His presence and so he stayed with Moses on the mountain until the time He handed over the ten commandments. He was holding unto in the secret place and so you and I must hold unto God.

For sure, God will evaluate our connection and as we get connected with God, He will prevent anything and everything that would want to separate us from Him. Understand how to know God for yourself and get real with God, knowing well that this is not a one-way stream. Just like Jacob saw the angels ascending and descending.

Have a relationship with God for He is raising a true bride without spot ready for the groom. Stay connected with God always and you will enter into a great blessing. Have God's directive over your life and all your relations. Do not allow your setbacks to disconnect you with God. Cut off all that does not please God by letting him prune you, so He can bring out your maximum. Don't let God remove you, for even with your condition his love towards you is still varied.

Have a Spiritual hunger for God by being connected to him. Be a branch that will produce fruit and you will not be cut off. Be connected to everything that flows out of God, for example favour, mercy, grace and eternal life. Just abide in Him and he will abide in you. I assure you that you will not fail but rather succeed in all your endeavour. Have a relationship with God so you can build together. Hear God, so that you distinguish from others, the voice of the master.

Samuel as a young lad was called by God and went to Eli who never knew at first it was God speaking. After a couple of the repeated scenario Eli was able to advice Samuel on what to say if he hears the voice again. Get, adjusted, connected and hear the voice of the Lord for yourself. Remember the bible says, in **Isaiah 33:22**, For the LORD is our judge, the LORD is our lawgiver, the LORD is our king; it is he who will save us. This can only be known in the secret place brethren when holding onto God alone.

**Isaiah 62:6** says, I have posted watchmen on your walls, Jerusalem; they will never be silent day or night. You who call on the LORD, give yourselves no rest.

The Lord is declaring His purpose of unceasing action to Zion as He associates Himself with the watchman whom he appoints and endows for purposes in some measure that resembles his own and working it out with constancy derived from Him.  So, these are watchmen and God's remembrance and their voices ought to be heard all the times.

The former metaphor is common in the old testament as a designation of the prophetic office just like in the new testament when the Holy Ghost was poured on the lowly as well as on the high, on the young and on the old and all of them prophesied and so has been extended to all Christians who believe.  God can make you a watchman if you avail yourself for the Master's use holding unto the master planner.  There is a solemn message committed to us by the fact that we are believers of Yeshua Hamashiach (Jesus Christ) and His works.  Our voices should be hard as we are holding unto God.

God has given us all faith that had to come with some responsibilities and of which no Christian can denude him/herself. We ought to warn the wicked to turn way from their wickedness, and blow the triumphed when we see the sword coming to catch ever gleaming on the horizon like when an army throw his spear.

Moreover, the outrider and the advance guard of who is coming is life or death. We should lift our voices and let the earth hear, Behold, our God comes to peal into the ears of men, sunken in the earthliness and dreaming of safety, the cry which may startle and save and ring out in glad tones to all who wearily ask watchman.

They will ask, what about the night, will it soon pass, so that the morning come. We must proclaim Yeshua (Jesus Christ) who came once to pay for our sins and so he is coming as a judge to bless and uphold righteousness. He will destroy the iniquity and so the watchman must do their work as they keep holding unto Jesus the Author and finisher of their faith.

## CHAPTER FOUR

## BEING PATIENT WITH GOD

In our **secret place** we need to address the issues that are our obstacles. Sometimes we have friend who give us wrong counsel. Know what and where God want you to go and live like Elijah, who was sent to Zarephath and was sent to specific place and the right time. You must understand the times just like the woman of Zarephath whose destiny was with Elijah for her earth to yield the produce. She was in the right place, at the right time and so was Elijah.

The book of **Luke 4:26** makes clear distinction saying, and yet Elijah was not sent to none of them, but to the Zarephath, in the land of Sidon to a woman who was a widow. This is not very pleasant thoughts to conjure, yet these are facts, but God was in His plan. Do not just go because others are going, you must know your right place, who are you going to meet or sent to and know the times. God told Abraham to leave his people and go to where God wanted him to be (Ur). May the peace of God in wherever you are, from within you, speak a blessing in that place.

My reader may I remind you that the earth yields fruit just like the scripture says, oh Earth, earth, earth, hear the word of the LORD! **Jeremiah 22:29**. We command the earth to release all the blessing of God's people in Yeshua's Mighty Name. We speak to the soil where they were born or where they have settled and are not making progress to see the goodness of the Lord, for the Lord will release them and we declare they are blessed and will make progress. It could be there are altars in the land or village, or county that you are in that speaks negative things and has made you to regret. Check for the Spiritual mapping and let God open your Spiritual eyes to see the heavenly opening so that a covenant can be established for you by God in Yeshua's Mighty Name.

It is imperative for you my reader to know the rule of God where your place is, the person who will be your connection and the right time. Even Jesus was born in Bethlehem in a manger and he had to leave since it was not his place and was taken to Nazareth. He had to go to where he was to be raised and there is need for us to understand the season and the appointed times. Command the earth saint and receive the love and increase of God, for it is His will.

Remember even when God asked Cain where his brother was after he had killed him. God said his blood was crying to God. This is to say that the earth has ears and may God release your break through while you are in your secret place in Yeshua's Mighty Name. When a man is operating under a curse he will not be blessed because the earth has been cursed.

Adam was cursed for not obeying God's instruction but listened to his wife but more so, the earth was cursed and it began to produce weed and thorns for its ears heard the one who spoke into existence and it obeyed. God said to Adam "Because you listened to your wife and ate fruit from the tree about which I commanded you, 'You must not eat from it, "Cursed is the ground because of you; through painful toil you will eat food from it all the days of your life. It will produce thorns and thistles for you, and you will eat the plants of the field **Genesis 3:17-18**.

In our **secret place** of prayer God will reveal and give us guideline and instructions of what we out to do. We are going to pray at this time my reader and ask God to heal us and all the areas that need healing. Even where we have followed the wrong counsel and we have gone astray we will ask God to forgive us. A good example is the advisor of King David. The word of God is so clear that his very counsellor was used of the enemy to try and destroy him.

If you read the book of **2Samuel 17:1** it says, "Moreover, Ahithophel said unto Absalom: 'Let me now pick twelve thousand men, and I will arise and pursue after David this night." He was a betrayal. He betrayed David and this made Absalom very happy. The name Ahithophel means unsalted. He was crafty like his name was crafted. Ahithophel was King David's advisor and his advice was accurate, but yet he betrayed him. He was the grandfather of Bath-Sheba.

When Absalom came, he lost his influence and left Absalom's camp and later hanged himself.

Please pray these prayers from the bottom of your heart saint of God and let the devil know that from now we bear the mark of our Lord Jesus Christ Yeshua Hamashiach and so he should not trouble us.  May the angel of vengeance arise and fight for us the Church in Yeshua's Mighty Name.

- Every **Ahithophel spirit** (betrayal) in our life falls down and die, **hang yourself** in Yeshua's Mighty Name.
- Therefore, every evil spirit summoned against me/you by our enemies, turn back your attack seven times against them.
- You our stolen blessings fight our enemies to death and come back to our life by fire in Yeshua's Name.
- Any unexplainable sickness, problem or evil arrow in our body vanish and return to sender in Yeshua's Name.
- Anyone challenging our breakthrough through by any means break down now and die in Yeshua's Name.

- Any masquerading (hidden) enemy behind my problems I command the heavenly serpent to bite and slap you in Jesus name.

- All our evil conspirators shall die in our place. The price has been paid for by Jesus Christ the son of God.

- Every power arranging for our execution this time of the year is executed in our place in Yeshua's Mighty Name.

- Oh!!! Lord elevates us this year by fire and let the devil know the saviour has been born and we can do all things through Christ who strengthens us.

- We break the evil pot of Egypt, fashioned against our Joseph (increase) in Yeshua's Name.

- May every pot break down and be consumed by the fire of God in Yeshua's Name. **Ezekiel 11** The bible says that the elder of the city sits at the gate plotting evil with cooking caldron (pot). Let the pot break into pieces now in Yeshua's Mighty Name.

- Any evil pot cooking our seed of success and greatness even this season fall down and perish in Yeshua's Name.
- Every incision mark in our body which was cut for protection known and unknown that hinders our progress be erased by the blood of the Lamb of God.
- Every witchcraft pot challenging our prosperity las a church be overthrown now in Yeshua's Mighty Name.
- Every diabolic intention of the enemy intended to destroy the body of Jesus Christ be roasted by fire.
- May every voice that speaks negative about us and be destroyed in Yeshua's Mighty Name.
- We command the dust of the earth to release lice, mosquitos to destroy all the wickedness according to **Exodus 8:16**. As he did in Egypt in Yeshua's Mighty Name.

The bible says, See, today I appoint you over nations and kingdoms to uproot and tear down, to destroy and overthrow, to build and to plant **Jeremiah 1:10**.

Every demonic challenge over our lives you are cursed with a curse and I command you to dry up from your root and be burned to ashes by the fire of the Holy Ghost In the name of Yeshua Hamashiach.

Therefore, be strong in the Lord and His mighty power **Ephesian 16:10**. I pray that the God of peace will give each one of us peace at all times and in every way even during challenging time. May God of hope fill you all with joy and peace as you trust in him, so that you may overflow with hope by the power of the Holy Spirit according to **Romans 15:13**. Know that we have a promise from God that cannot not be altered. The Scriptures has made us to know that the people of God will leave in a peaceful dwelling places in secure homes, in undisturbed places of rest according to **Isaiah 32:18**.

May the Lord help us to number our days so that we can enjoy His promised benefits. Let's remember that the devil is roaring like a lion looking for whom to devour.

So, what should the righteous do when the foundation is destroyed? According to **Psalms 11:3**. When we engage God through prayer on our side and when faith secures the fulfilment of the promise, nothing can cause us to flight, however cruel and mighty our enemies can be?

With a sling and a stone, David had smitten a giant before whom the whole hosts of Israel were trembling, and the Lord, who delivered him from the uncircumcised Philistine, could surely deliver him from King Saul and his myrmidons. There is no such word as "impossibility" in the language of faith; that martial grace knows how to fight and conquer, but she knows not how to flee. Is it possible that the foundations of religion should be destroyed?

Can God be in so long a sleep, I mean, so long a lethargy (tired), as patiently to permit the ruins thereof? If he looks on, and yet does not see these foundations when being destroyed, where then is his omniscience? If he sees it, and cannot help it, where then is his omnipotence? If he sees it, and He can help it, and will not, where then is his goodness and mercy? Martha said to Jesus "Lord, if you have been here, my brother would not have died **John 11:21**.

Nonetheless, many will say, were God effectually present in the world with his aforesaid attributes, surely the foundations had not been destroyed. We have an express promise of Christ that the gates of hell shall not prevail against the church **Matthew 16:18**.

Nevertheless, the foundation of God stands sure, having this seal, the Lord knows them that are his period! In our secret place we will say like Joshua, now fear the Lord and serve him with all faithfulness **Joshua 24:14-15**. So, in our humility and brokenness we should surrender to God and confess our sins and ask Him for forgiveness.

Whatever we ask in our secret place God in heaven will hear and will heal us from our unfaithfulness. The civil foundation of a nation or people, is their laws and constitutions.

The order and power that's among them, that's the foundation of a people; and when once this foundation is destroyed, What can the righteous do? What can any man do, if there be not a foundation of government left among men even in the Kingdom of God? What can the wisest in the world or the best builders do in such a case? There is no help nor answer in such a case but **Psalm 82:5** says, the 'gods' know nothing, they understand nothing. They walk about in darkness; all the foundations of the earth are shaken. Until now, God keeps his course still, and he is where he was and as he was, without variableness or shadow of turning.

During the time of prophet Jeremiah, he told the wicked of his degenerate age, that. If you do not listen, I will weep in secret because of your pride; my eyes will weep bitterly, overflowing with tears, because the LORD's flock will be taken captive **Jeremiah 13:17**. Imagine him saying to his people his soul should weep in secret.

Indeed, sometimes sin comes to such a height, that this is almost all the godly can do, to get into a corner, a secret place and bewail the general pollutions of the age.

I say it again brethren, if the foundations be destroyed, what can the righteous do? In such a dismal day of national confusion our eyes have seen, when foundations of government were destroyed, economy crumble, churches shut down and so forth and all hurled into confusion. When it is like this with a people, "What can the righteous do? Yes, this they may, and should do, "**fast and pray.**"

There is yet a God in heaven to be sought to, when a people's deliverance is thrown beyond the help of human policy or power. Now is the fit time to make their appeal to God, as the words clearly states that the Lord is in his holy temple, the Lord's throne is in heaven; in which words God is presented sitting in heaven as a temple, for their encouragement, I conceive, in such a desperate state of affairs, to direct their prayers for deliverance.

And certainly, this has been the engine that has been instrumental, above any, to restore any poor nation, family, church etc again, and set it upon the foundation of that lawful government or leadership from which it had so dangerously departed.

At this time the Lord will roar from Zion and thunder from Jerusalem, the earth and the sky will tremble, but the Lord will be a refuge for His people, a stronghold for the people of Israel **Joel 3:16**. In our secret place, the Lord will remind us that He has redeemed us and saved us by grace and not by works rest any man boasts. He has already set a table for his bride before her enemies and anoint her head with oil, her cup overflows.

God will restore everything and all we need is to rejoice in the Lord. The God whom we trust will release grace and strength to us day by day. Until challenge strikes you may not know how strong you are. We have been bought with a price saints and we shall obtain an everlasting joy for God has promised to make a covenant of peace and has called the evil to cease out of their land according to the book of **Ezekiel 34:25**.

Trust you me our redeemer lives and so we shall live to declare his goodness in the land of the living. You are not permitted to fail and whatever you lay your hands will prosper. I declare and decree that God will revive every area that needs to be revived in your life and every agent of Satan and wickedness will stay off your life in Jesus Mighty Name.

We will finish strong because for sure the Lord will find faith on the earth upon His return for there are His remnants. We will continue to feed our mind with the word of God for the Spirit will give us life. We shall trust in the Lord and will not lean on our understanding. The word of God are spirit and life and spirit give life and this will nourish and enrich your soul. Let's be thankful to God for a thankful heart is not only the greatest virtue but the parent of all virtues.

This is to say God will bless you and not rest until your enthronement comes.

Never forget that you are a loyal diadem and you will eat the riches of the gentiles and in their glory, you shall boast yourself in Yeshua's Mighty Name. Rejoice for we are going through a period of sanitizing our spirit men so we come out thorough and properly moulded.

In **Luke 9:62**, This scripture affirms to us that there is no one who puts his hand to the plough and looks back is fit for the kingdom of God." The sense of this translation is that putting your hand to the plough is a symbol of following Jesus, and if you have started "ploughing", you should not look back. Never regret about the world pleasures, honours and wealth. Do the work of the one who has called you. Whatever you do no turning back brethren. Be focused unto the finishing line.

## CHAPTER FIVE

## GOD WATCHES OVER HIS PEOPLE

In this chapter we will be looking at a number of Scriptures, to strengthen us in our walk with God. As we continue to watch and wait in our **secret place** by the power of the Holy Spirit, who is our comforter he will enable us to endure till the end. My reader these notes were written as I meditated in the scriptures, and you as you read through as the spirit of God enlightens you, fill free to take notes as this is a bible study chapter if you like.

In the book of **Roman 8:35-39**, the bible says, who shall separate us from the love of Christ? Shall trouble or hardship or persecution or famine or nakedness or danger or sword? As it is written: "For your sake we face death all day long; we are considered as sheep to be slaughtered." No, in all these things we are more than conquerors through him who loved us. For I am convinced that neither death nor life, neither angels nor demons, neither the present nor the future, nor any powers, neither height nor depth, nor anything else in all creation, will be able to separate us from the love of God that is in Christ Jesus our Lord.

*Note: Allow me to make this remark, the devil does not fear a big church, or bank account, he fears a United Church, a united Nation or a united Family etc. It's only God who can fill any void and vacuum spaces by the power of His blood through His son Jesus Christ the Messiah. Church there is hope and purpose in Christ Jesus.*

**Psalms 37:24** say, though he may stumble, he will not fall, for the LORD upholds him with his hand. Be encouraged that whatever challenge you may be going through, focus your eye in the Lord. Also, if you read the scriptures in the book of **2 Thessalonians 3:3**, the bible says, "But the Lord is faithful, and he will strengthen you and protect you from the evil one." He will establish you and guard you against the evil one."

**Ephesians 1:21** affirms that He exerted when he raised Christ from the dead and seated him at his right hand in the heavenly realms, far above all rule and authority, power and dominion, and every name that is invoked, not only in the present age but also in the one to come.

*Note: What am trying to say is the word of God is settled in heaven. Fear not for our King reigns forever. Focus on Him and have attention to the lessons that are in this pandemic challenge or whatever situation that you are in. This also means that Christ is the foundation and there is no other foundation that can stand.*

According to **1 Corinthians 3:10-15**, bible affirms that, By the grace God has given me, I laid a foundation as a wise builder, and someone else is building on it. But each one should build with care. For no one can lay any foundation other than the one already laid, which is Jesus Christ. If anyone builds on this foundation using gold, silver, costly stones, wood, hay or straw, their work will be shown for what it is, because the Day will bring it to light.

It will be revealed with fire, and the fire will test the quality of each person's work.  If what has been built survives, the builder will receive a reward.  If it is burned up, the builder will suffer loss but yet will be saved even though only as one escaping through the flames.

*There are different materials that one can use to build. Some use gold, silver or precious stones while others use wood, hay and straw.  This is a quick way, it's big but cannot stand the test. Every material that is used will determine whether the foundation will stand the test of time.  Can what we are building stand during temptations and challenges or will it collapse and be consumed when it's passed through fire?  We should have intimacy with God and we should not depend on our wealth or intellectuals for that will not safe us. Only the word of God shall stand the testing.*

The bible says in **1Phillipians 1:3-6**, I thank my God every time I remember you.  In all my prayers for all of you, I always pray with joy because of your partnership in the gospel from the first day until now, being confident of this, that he who began a good work in you will carry it on to completion until the day of Christ Jesus. The book of **Psalms 84 :11** says, For the LORD God is a sun and shield; the LORD bestows favour and honour; no good thing does he withhold from those whose walk is blameless.

*Note: This is to say, He is God all by Himself, He is supreme, omnipotent, omniscience and no one can be compared to He who spoke into existence. We therefore loose immunity and defence in every home, nation to the rich and poor and to four corners of the earth North, South, West and East in Yeshua's Name. You, demonic virus, and every other challenge, we bind you and send you to hell fire by the authority of God's word in Yeshua Name.*

*I tell you the truth, you can say to this mountain, 'May you be lifted up and thrown into the sea,' and it will happen. But you must really believe it will happen and have no doubt in your heart Mark 11:23. We take authority and close all borders of every Nation with the blood of Yeshua that does not lose its power that this plague and every other challenge will not destroy God's children. We dismantle, we crush, we defeat and we kill this virus and every other diabolic satanic plan as the angels of defence help to take over in Jesus Mighty Name. As the children of the promise we will remain in the holy sanctuary until we win.*

*We will close our doors in our secret place and not allow any distraction that brings defeat to derive near our camp and this season will also pass.*

The book of **1Peter 1:3-5** has made it clear, by saying, Praise be to the God and Father of our Lord Jesus Christ! In his great mercy he has given us new birth into a living hope through the resurrection of Jesus Christ from the dead, and into an inheritance that can never perish, spoil or fade. This inheritance is kept in heaven for you, who through faith are shielded by God's power until the coming of the salvation that is ready to be revealed in the last time.

**Nahum 1:7** say, The LORD is good, a refuge in times of trouble. He cares for those who trust in him.

*Note:*

*So, we rebuke fear and release the Spirit of faith for God is our defence and He is our strong tower. No wonder Job said his days are shifter than a runner. Jesus has overcome the world over two thousand years ago. For He overcame the events and the environment.*

*This Means He overcame sickness and diseases, all deadly viruses, in the world and this is settled in His word which will never be violated by no powers even in the world to come.*

**Psalms 121:3-8** say, He will not let your foot slip he who watches over you will not slumber; indeed, he who watches over Israel will neither slumber nor sleep. The LORD watches over you, the LORD is your shade at your right hand; the sun will not harm you by day, nor the moon by night. The LORD will keep you from all harm he will watch over your life; the LORD will watch over your coming and going both now and forevermore.

*Note:*

*This means that our feet will be firm and immoveable in God's protection as the hills themselves. It is one of his own sweet promises, that he will give his angels charge over every child of his, and that nothing shall be able to harm them. But, how immeasurably beyond even the untiring wings of angels is the love promised here that love which engages to protect us from every danger, as a hen gathers her chickens under her wings.*

**John 7: 37-38** also encourages us that, on the last and greatest day of the festival, Jesus stood and said in a loud voice, let anyone who is thirsty come to me and drink. Whoever believes in me, as Scripture has said, rivers of living water will flow from within them.

*Note:*

*WE ARE HEAVENLY DEFENDED, FORTFIED, AND WE ARE PROTECTED, SECURED AND SAFEGUARDED*

*AND THERE IS NO DEVIL THAT CAN CHANGE IT IN YESHUA'S MIGHTY NAME.*

No wonder **Psalms 91:1-2** affirms that, whoever dwells in the shelter of the Most High will rest in the shadow of the Almighty. I will say of the LORD, "He is my refuge and my fortress, my God, in whom I trust."

Besides, **Psalms 91:5-8** says that, you will not fear the terror of night, nor the arrow that flies by day, nor the pestilence that stalks in the darkness, nor the plague that destroys at midday. A thousand may fall at your side, ten thousand at your right hand, but it will not come near you. You will only observe with your eyes and see the punishment of the wicked.

Still, **Psalms 91:11-13** postulates that, he will command his angels concerning you to guard you in all your ways; they will lift you up in their hands, so that you will not strike your foot against a stone. You will tread on the lion and the cobra; you will trample the great lion and the serpent.

*Note: At the end of it all God is all what matters brethren. Fear Him for the fear of God is the beginning of wisdom. See how all Nations have stood still. Fear God.*

*May God help us to pray with understanding that when we as His children, we unite and pray corporately God will send deliverance.*

## 2Timothy 1:7

Brethren fear not, worry not, For God hath not given us the spirit of fear; but of power, and of love, and of a sound mind. For those who know their Gods shall do exploits.

*Note: Do not be afraid of death for it is the vehicle to take us to heaven but not by corona virus for we and our household are divinely protected. The blood of Yeshua has taken over. Therefore, fear not but pray for the earnest prayer of the righteous avails much. Never be ignorant of the devices of the enemy.*

*It's time for the vulnerability of everyone, uncertainty of life, scarcity of hope but above all credibility of the bible. Amen!*

**Isaiah 41:15**

"See, I will make you into a threshing sledge, new and sharp, with many teeth. You will thresh the mountains and crush them, and reduce the hills to chaff."

*Note: Authority is a tool that God has released to His children for use at all times.*

*Let us all do stock or Evaluate yourselves and check if we qualify to exercise the authority released by God to us.*

**2 Timothy 1:12-14**, the scriptures tells us,

For which course I also suffer these things: nevertheless, I am not ashamed: for I know whom I have believed, and am persuaded that he is able to keep that which I have committed unto him against that day. Hold fast the form of sound words, which thou hast heard of me, in faith and love which is in Christ Jesus. That good thing which was committed unto thee keep by the Holy Ghost which dwelleth in us.

## Isaiah 43:2

When you pass through the waters, I will be with you; and when you pass through the rivers, they will not sweep over you. When you walk through the fire, you will not be burned; the flames will not set you ablaze.

*Note: Elijah went through it and even thought he was the only prophet left who had not worshiped Baal. God told him, Nonetheless, I have reserved seven thousand in Israel, all whose knees have not bowed to Baal and whose mouths have not kissed him."1Kings 19:18.*

*God prepare the church for your coming glory and give us a supper abundance of your victory in Jesus Mighty Name.*

## Isaiah 26:20-21

Go, my people, enter your rooms and shut the doors behind you; hide yourselves for a little while until his wrath has passed by. See, the LORD is coming out of his dwelling to punish the people of the earth for their sins. The earth will disclose the blood shed on it; the earth will conceal its slain no longer.

*Note: Praise God for He has delivered us from the snare of the devourer before the time. The church is matching on with great power and authority all will see and know how great is our God. As it is, I am persuaded and so shall it be in Yeshua's Mighty Name.*

**2 Chronicles 7:13-15** has clearly said to God's people, "When I shut up the heavens so that there is no rain, or command locusts to devour the land or send a plague among my people, if my people, who are called by my name, will humble themselves and pray and seek my face and turn from their wicked ways, then I will hear from heaven, and I will forgive their sin and will heal their land. Now my eyes will be open and my ears attentive to the prayers offered in this place.

*Note: Brethren, I was in Kenya when Locust flew into our land, those who followed me on Facebook will bear me witness.*

*The pestilence (locust) has come for real, deadly diseases, but it's still not yet time <u>though too close</u>. Jesus Said, no one except the father knows the hour. Let us just keep preparing ourselves for the second coming of our Lord and saviour Jesus Christ the Messiah (Yeshua Hamashiach). Its near than when we began. Be Real and Pray!*

According to **3 John 2-4** the bible says, Dear friend, I pray that you may enjoy good health and that all may go well with you, even as your soul is getting along well. It gave me great joy when some believers came and testified about your faithfulness to the truth, telling how you continue to walk in it. I have no greater joy than to hear that my children are walking in the truth.

Also, in the book of **Proverb 19:16 & 23,** Whoever keeps the commandments, keeps their life, but whoever shows contempt for their ways will die. The fear of the LORD leads to life; then one rests content, untouched by trouble.

*Note: This is to say obedience to the Almighty God's commandments, will be rewarded by a long and happy life in this world, an adumbration of the blessedness that awaits the righteous in the world to come. The righteous even in the hour of darkness shall be free from fear but must obey the instructions.*

Nevertheless, **Isaiah 14:27 say**, For the LORD Almighty has purposed, and who can thwart him? His hand is stretched out, and who can turn it back?

*Note: There is nothing that can pass but what God alone has purposed, and everything he has purposed must come to pass. No one can alter not even the most powerful monarch, or most powerful armies, or the most refined councils of men, or the greatest politicians on earth and when His hand is stretched out, no one can turn it back whatsoever.*

*No one can frustrate the plan of God in our lives but if we remain in our secret place seeking His plan and will for our life.*

That is why **Isaiah 26:3** has made us know that He will keep in perfect peace those whose minds are steadfast, because they trust in you. We are encouraged in **2 Chronicles 20:15** which says, He said, Listen, King Jehoshaphat and all who live in Judah and Jerusalem! This is what the LORD says to you, do not be afraid or discouraged because of this vast army. For the battle is not yours, but God's.

In **Exodus 12:12-13** God spoke to Moses saying, on that same night I will pass through Egypt and strike down every firstborn of both people and animals, and I will bring judgment on all the god of Egypt. I am the Lord The blood will be a sign for you on the houses where you are, and when I see the blood, I will pass over you. No destructive plague will touch you when I strike Egypt.

*Note: The Lord makes all things new to those whom he delivers from the bondage of Satan, and takes them to himself to be his people. Any time when He does this is to them the beginning of a new life. The angel of the Lord, when destroying the first-born of the Egyptians, would pass over the houses marked by the blood of the lamb. Their safety and deliverance were not a reward of their own righteousness, but the gift of mercy. Of this they were reminded, and by this ordinance they were taught, that all blessings came to them through the shedding and sprinkling of blood.*

**Proverbs 21:10** says the wicked crave evil; their neighbours get no mercy from them.

*Note: Just like He did with the children of Israel, any door that had blood on its post the angel of death passed by. After the battle the children of Israel came to Moses and said we have counted and none is missing. Even now the blood of Yeshua the messiah is enough to protect us and our households and none of us will die*

The bible makes us to understand that God has made Himself so clear when He said that "I will have mercy on whom I have mercy, and I will have compassion on whom I have compassion" according to **Romans 9:15.**

*Note:*

*Then, I urges you brethren, go into your house and wait there for a little while until the Lord finishes His mission. When He is done, He will show up and vindicate His children publicly. Once again, I am so persuaded that; with their own sword (enemies) they will kill each other until they all die.*

*Psalms 34:1b*

I will extol the LORD at all times; his praise will always be on my lips.

*Note: Let us pray that our mouth will be full of praise and not complains, and pray that we all learn how to praise God at all times regardless of all the challenges, we will trust Him and we will overcome for this is also going to pass.*

## Acts 19:13-16

Some Jews who went around driving out evil spirits tried to invoke the name of the Lord Jesus over those who were demon possessed. They would say, "In the name of the Jesus whom Paul preaches, I command you to come out." Seven sons of Sceva, a Jewish chief priest, were doing this. One day the evil spirit answered them, "Jesus I know, and Paul I know about, but who are you? Then the man who had the evil spirit jumped on them and overpowered them all. He gave them such a beating that they ran out of the house naked and bleeding.

*Note: Please as we keep putting on the whole armour of God examine yourself before you begin to attack the devil. Do you have the authority to destroy or you are imitating others? Be yourself and do not joke with the word authority for the enemy is scared of it. The devil is a rebellious devil and will not tolerate you not to submit to his authority. Take this seriously and free from the devil and he will free from you. Exercise your authority in God and this corona virus is a demon that need to hear you speak and submit because of the authority that you and I carry. We should not joke with the devil. Heed to instructions and then pray. Resist him and he will run with haste.*

The book of **James 4:7** says submit yourselves, then, to God. Resist the devil, and he will flee from you.

**Luke 10:17-19** say, the seventy-two returned with joy and said, "Lord, even the demons submit to us in your name. He replied, I saw Satan fall like lightning from heaven. I have given you authority to trample on snakes and scorpions and to overcome all the power of the enemy, nothing will harm you.

The bible says in **Matthew 18:9-11,** And if your eye causes you to stumble, gouge it out and throw it away. It is better for you to enter life with one eye than to have two eyes and be thrown into the fire of hell. See that you do not despise one of these little ones. For I tell you that their angels in heaven always see the face of my Father in heaven.

*Note: All what we think we know and have is all vanity of vanity, guard your heart beloved and know how to submit to the word of God. This is only a reminder that soon and very soon there is an end of everything. One of the assurances we have is when he is revealed we shall be like Him.*

**Psalms 32:8 say** I will instruct you and teach you in the way you should go; I will counsel you with my loving eye on you.

*Note: These are the promises of God and many more as we walk in His light brethren. Prepare for eternity for its coming soon. Listen to the instruction from the Holy Spirit who is our helper. He will direct us in all we want to do and that which will please the Master.*

**Psalms 41:1-3**

Blessed are those who have regard for the weak; the LORD delivers them in times of trouble. The LORD protects and preserves them they are counted among the blessed in the land he does not give them over to the desire of their foes.

The LORD sustains them on their sickbed and restores them from their bed of illness.

**Isaiah 49:15**

Can a mother forget the baby at her breast and have no compassion on the child she has borne? Though she may forget, I will not forget you!

**Proverbs 3:5-6**

Trust in the LORD with all your heart and lean not on your own understanding; in all your ways submit to him, and he will make your paths straight.

*Note: Therefore, fear not and do not be afraid for God will be with us till the end. What is the quality of your mind? It will determine what the world will become. You are the world and so, trust not your money, Family or church but in the Lord God Almighty. Know God for yourself. Remember we walk by faith not by sight. We are mighty warrior, men and women who knows God and believes that the price was paid for on the cross of calvary.*

*We are more than conquerors in Christ Jesus for He gave us dominion over all. It's our own responsibility to manage and develop the goal that God had for man. We are victorious and not victim and even this demon of covid19 will not come near our dwelling in Yeshua's Mighty Name.*

*LET'S LOOK AT SOME OF THE REASONS WHY SIN HAS ENTERED THE HEARTS OF MEN AND SO CONTAMINATING THE WORLD AND THE CHURCH AS A WHOLE:*

Please read these scriptures with an open mind my reader, and I trust that they will be helpful. If you are able to write down any questions and have a meeting with one or two of your family or friends and answer them if possible. Iron sharpens iron my reader. I pray that you glean something from this and all the scriptures given.

## Leviticus 11:13-19

These are the birds you are to regard as unclean and not eat because they are unclean: the eagle, the vulture, the black vulture, the red kite, any kind of black kite, any kind of raven, the horned owl, the screech owl, the gull, any kind of hawk, the little owl, the cormorant, the great owl, the white owl, the desert owl, the osprey, the stork, any kind of heron, the hoopoe and the bat.

## Isaiah 66:17

"Those who consecrate and purify themselves to go into the gardens, following one who is among those who eat the flesh of pigs, rats and other unclean things they will meet their end together with the one they follow," declares the LORD.

## Leviticus 20:15-20

If a man has sexual relations with an animal, he is to be put to death, and you must kill the animal. If a woman approaches an animal to have sexual relations with it, kill both the woman and the animal.

They are to be put to death; their blood will be on their own heads (read to verse 20).

## Leviticus 3:17

This is a lasting ordinance for the generations to come, wherever you live: You must not eat any fat or any blood.

## Genesis 7:2-8

Take with you seven pairs of every kind of clean animal, a male and its mate, and one pair of every kind of unclean animal, a male and its mate, and also seven pairs of every kind of bird, male and female, to keep their various kinds alive throughout the earth. Seven days from now I will send rain on the earth for forty days and forty nights, and I will wipe from the face of the earth every living creature I have made." and Noah did all that the LORD commanded him. Noah was six hundred years old when the floodwaters came on the earth. And Noah and his sons and his wife and his sons' wives entered the ark to escape the waters of the flood. Pairs of clean and unclean animals, of birds and of all creatures that move along the ground,

**Mark 8:2-3**

I have compassion for these people; they have already been with me three days and have nothing to eat. If I send them home hungry, they will collapse on the way, because some of them have come a long distance.

*NOTE: As the Lord had mercy before, may He break the yoke of any diabolic satanic agenda in every Nation and vindicate His people in Jesus Mighty Name. Remember repentance is vital and the message of the cross which is salvation. The love of the father is so great, the world does know us, so it does not know Him. We are his children (1John 3:1).*

**John13:10-11**

Jesus answered, "Those who have had a bath need only to wash their feet; their whole body is clean. And you are clean, though not every one of you."

For he knew who was going to betray him, and that was why he said not everyone was clean.

## Leviticus 13:6-7

On the seventh day the priest is to examine them again, and if the sore has faded and has not spread in the skin, the priest shall pronounce them clean; it is only a rash. They must wash their clothes, and they will be clean. But if the rash does spread in their skin after they have shown themselves to the priest to be pronounced clean, they must appear before the priest again.

## Exodus 30:17-21

Then the LORD said to Moses, "Make a bronze basin, with its bronze stand, for washing. Place it between the tent of meeting and the altar, and put water in it. Aaron and his sons are to wash their hands and feet with water from it. Aaron and his sons are to wash their hands and feet with water from it. Whenever they enter the tent of meeting, they shall wash with water so that they will not die. Also, when they approach the altar to minister by presenting a food offering to the LORD, they shall wash their hands and feet so that they will not die.  This is to be a lasting ordinance for Aaron and his descendants for the generations to come.

If we read the scriptures, we will learn that touching anything unclean makes us unclean.  So, **Leviticus 15:1-20**.  The LORD said to Moses and Aaron, "Speak to the Israelites and say to them: 'When any man has an unusual bodily discharge, such a discharge is unclean, whether it continues flowing from his body or is blocked, it will make him unclean.  This is how his discharge will bring about uncleanness.  Any bed the man with a discharge lies on will be unclean, and anything he sits on will be unclean.

Anyone who touches his bed must wash their clothes and bathe with water, and they will be unclean till evening.  Whoever sits on anything that the man with a discharge sat on must wash their clothes and bathe with water, and they will be unclean till evening.  Whoever touches the man who has a discharge must wash their clothes and bathe with water, and they will be unclean till evening.   Read this scripture to verse 20.

**Revelation 19:8-14**

Fine linen, bright and clean, was given her to wear.  (Fine linen stands for the righteous acts of God's holy people.) Then the angel said to me, write this: Blessed are those who are invited to the wedding supper of the Lamb! And he added, "These are the true words of God."

*NOTE: This is to say only cleanliness is of God brethren, and only clean people will inherit the Kingdom of God.  Wash, wash, wash is all about cleanliness which is second to God. Let's all go back to the Manual the Holy word of God and stop this diplomatic or tactful method we are using to manipulate the truth.*

*Let's Clean our inner being first and then we can do the job in unison. In my own thinking I am convinced that this is not a preaching time but Prayer time.*

*I hope this will help us as a people to meditate on what God has to say at this end time. I believe if we are all able to read these scriptures and go to our knees in prayer on daily basis God will hear us and will heal families, the Church and then our Nations will be restored in Yeshua's Mighty Name. I have put on some Notes which you can add as you read this book and get new revelation.*

*We will repent for all our sins and the iniquity that we have done and the world as a whole and for sure there will be a performance as we use the Word Yeshua Hamashiach (Jesus the mighty one of Israel) our only help that we know. We ask for mercy and if we trust on Him, He will give us another chance as he releases his hand of mercy over all Nations in His Mighty Name. His word is new every single moment and I believe He will give us another chance.*

# CHAPTER SIX

## SUPERNATURAL TRANSFORMATION

When God want to bless you in a supernatural way no power can stop it just like in the case of Mordecai. It is a very powerful case study to give us some intuition. Moreover, the bible in **Ester 6:1-5**, That night the king could not sleep; so, he ordered the book of the chronicles, the record of his reign, to be brought in and read to him. It was found recorded there that Mordecai had exposed Bigthana and Teresh, two of the king's officers who guarded the doorway, who had conspired to assassinate King Xerxes. Mordecai heard the two men discussing a plot about assassinating the king and he reported it.  He was remembered by his deeds.

"What honour and recognition has Mordecai received for this?" the king asked. "Nothing has been done for him," his attendants answered.  The king said, "Who is in the court?" Now Haman had just entered the outer court of the palace to speak to the king about impaling Mordecai on the pole he had set up for him.

His attendants answered, "Haman is standing in the court." "Bring him in," the king ordered.  "Verse 10 says, Go at once," the king commanded Haman.  "Get the robe and the horse and do just as you have suggested for Mordecai the Jew, who sits at the king's gate.

Do not neglect anything you have recommended."  So, Haman got the robe and the horse. He robed Mordecai, and led him on horseback through the city streets, proclaiming before him, "This is what is done for the man the king delights to honour!"  You will be remembered by your name and deeds in Yeshua's Mighty Name.

It's time to come out of Lo debar the place of lack and enter into the Lords rest.  Dine with the King for your oil cannot touch anyone else just rise above the storm like an eagle. None, no one can take your place and your oil will defile gravity for your sake.  It will not pour out of the jar till you arrive in the scene in Yeshua's Name.

We are coming out of Lo Debar supernaturally in Yeshua's Name. I love this scripture, **Exodus 22:18** says: Suffer not for a witch to live! By the time we get to chapter 7, Haman is on top of the gallows he made for Mordecai. We must come out of Lo debar the place of lack, want, discrimination sickness, diseases, pandemic of every form and shape. We cannot give our enemy the devil a chance for we have been promised life eternal if we overcome.

In **Deuteronomy11:13-15** the bible say, so if you faithfully obey the commands I am giving you today to love the LORD your God and to serve him with all your heart and with all your soul then I will send rain on your land in its season, both autumn and spring rains, so that you may gather in your grain, new wine and olive oil. I will provide grass in the fields for your cattle, and you will eat and be satisfied. God had a plan for Mordecai and was willing to release rain to him.

Therefore, the same plot the enemy has made for us they will fall into it in Yeshua's Name.

Mordecai was certain that his father God will never fail him. Our enemies will always laugh first but when we begin to laugh it shall be permanent.

So, we have the right to tell the devil you fought us yesterday but today we have escaped from the snare of the enemy in Yeshua's Name. We must achieve our destiny when divine impact takes place. Supernaturally God brought Mordecai to palace.

In **Esther 9:1**. The scriptures say, now in the twelfth month, that is, the month of Adar, on the thirteenth day, the time came for the king's com\mand and his decree to be executed. On the day that the enemies of the Jews had hoped to overpower them, the opposite occurred, in that the Jews themselves overpowered those who hated them. This is on the thirteenth day of the twelfth month, so about 9 months have passed since chapter 8. This is the day that Haman had chosen by casting the lot to eradicate the Jews, and on which all the enemies of the Jews were hoping to do just that. God is not partial and does not respect any persons.

Also, in **Esther 9:2-5** the bibles tell us that the Jews gathered together in their cities throughout all the provinces of King Ahasuerus to lay hands on those who sought their harm. And no one could withstand them, because fear of them fell upon all people. Thus, the Jews defeated all their enemies with the stroke of the sword, with slaughter and destruction, and did what they pleased with those who hated them. The devil only plans for destruction and any one waiting for negative report, it will not come whatever they meant for evil God will turn it around for your good Yeshua's Name.

Similarly, that's why all these series of events show that God is with His people, even when His presence is not actively recognized or seen. Against impossible odds, and through a set of amazing, miraculous coincidences, Esther accomplished her mission. Proud Haman was put to death, while Esther's humble and patient uncle Mordecai, receives the position of being second in command over the entire empire. He was supernaturally transformed from being a beggar to an heir. Mordecai encouraged them to continue celebrating this feast of gladness till to date, Jews still celebrate Purim today.

In **Esther 9: 6**, The scripture lists all the names of the ten sons of Haman and visually expresses the idea that these enemies of Israel had been set apart for destruction. First, this list of names, and the fact that these men are put to death, is a fulfilment of prophecy. In **Exodus 17:14** and **Deuteronomy 25:17-19,** God says that he will have war with the Amalekites from generation to generation until they are destroyed.

In the book of **Esther 10:3**. The bible says, for Mordecai the Jew God turned his story around and he became was second to King Ahasuerus, and was great among the Jews and well received by the multitude of his brethren, seeking the good of his people and speaking peace to all his countrymen. Our God is faithful and will do that for us too, if we follow His ways, and wait for His timing, and trust Him with our life and our decisions. No threat of the devil should make our faith in God waiver.

He has promised and He will fulfil His promises. We are His children hidden under his pavilion and divinely protected. No evil can manifest their intention over your life in Jesus Mighty Name.

If you read the book of **Galatians 6:17**, the bible says, from now, let no man trouble me for I bare the mark of the Lord. I mentioned this earlier but I repeats it again saints. Am excited that am not a beggar but an heir with the King of kings Yeshua Himself. We shall not open ourselves for trouble because Jesus came to destroy the works of the devil. We are destined for greatness.

The book of **Deuteronomy 28:13**, we hear, And the Lord shall make us the head and not the tail, above and not beneath if we hearken unto the commandments of the Lord our God which he commanded us this day to observe and to do them. No devil can stop you from excelling. No Jezebel spirit will stop you in Yeshua's Name.

The bible says in the book of **1Samuel 16:1-13,** Samuel went to the house of Jesse to anoint a king because God had rejected Saul. When Samuel got to the house of Jesse, he brought seven of his sons before the prophet and God said no. Eliab came and Samuel saw his appearance because men look at the outward appearance but God said no. Abinadab came, Shammah and Jesse made seven of his sons to pass by Prophet Samuel and God said no. Then Samuel asked Jesse are these the only sons you have? There is still the youngest who is tendering sheep. Samuel said, send for him, for we shall not sit down until he arrives.

David came but he was ruddy (health looking) with a fine appearance and handsome features. The Lord spoke to Samuel and said arise and anoint him for he is the one. Samuel took the horn and anointed him and from then hence forth the spirit of the Lord came upon David with power and Samuel went to Ramah. God must raise a Samuel for you and me for He is a speciality who picks up the zeros and makes them heroes.

He picks you from grass to grace and floor to top. When it's your time God will supernaturally transform you against all odds like he did for David. Stop mourning about your past for God is of present. If He wanted your past then we could be leaving yesterday if it was great. He has a wonderful program for us all. God knew he had a king in David and so he had to make sure he is enthroned.

**Jeremiah 29:11** says, For I know the plans I have for you, declares the LORD, plans to prosper you and not to harm you, plans to give you hope and a future. Before the foundations of the earth God had put all things in place. My reader, let me give us an insight a little bit of Elijah the prophet. All what he did could only happen if one is and has been waiting in a **secret place**.

In the book of **1 Kings 18**, we read, Therefore, Elijah confronted the evil king, Ahab, about being the cause of problems for the people of Israel. Elijah challenges Ahab to a demonstration of his deity, Baal, versus the God of Elijah at Mount Carmel. The challenge is to offer sacrifices to their respective deities and see which starts a fire to prove their divinity. Ahab's prophets prayed for hours to Baal but nothing happened.

In **verse 30,** when Elijah's turn came, he boldly repaired the altar making sure that he represented the twelve tribes of Israel and said to the people fill everywhere with water to display his supreme trust in God to start a fire despite being wet. They did and Elijah knowing his God well was ready to display His splendour. He lifted his eyes unto the Lord and said, O Lord, God of Abraham, Isaac and Israel, let it be known today that you are God in Israel and that I am your servant and have done all these things at your command. Answer me, by fire, O Lord, answer me, so these people will know that you, O Lord, are God, and that you are turning their hearts back again."

God sent down a fire that completely sacked the water and consumed everything in flames and the people of Israel rejoiced with a new found faith in God. The fire was followed by rain ending the long drought, further showing God's grace.

The Israelites lost faith in Ahab and followed Elijah's guidance in trusting and recognizing God and his sovereignty.

Remember at some stage Elijah had almost given up but God promised him he will; be with him for he has hidden seven thousand men who have not worshiped Baal **1 Kings 19**. Elijah could have gone through physical and emotional hardship just like we all do. What we think is not always what God thinks, even if in our minds it is a "good plan" At this very point Elijah experienced the crushing and the disappointment that God seemed not to keep his part of the bargain.

The prophet assumed that if they won the victory on Mount Carmel that God would therefore act to bring about a change in the people, but it didn't happen. Resentment against God began to descend on Elijah's heart so that in despair he finally said, let me die. It's not worth living. God, you've disappointed me too deeply. If I can give as much of my life and my heart as I have to you and have it turn out like this, I don't want to live anymore because flesh can speak anything.

Large amounts of stress will cause you to physically be tired and sleep much and this is an indicator to push to renew one's hope in God, or better yet, pray for God to renew your hope. God did not rebuke his servant but first attends to his other needs. What a good God, Saviour who cares about every aspect of our lives. Even when we are self-centred me, myself and I, he understands our weakness and so when we call him, he answers.

God sends what His servant needs to be restored starting with his physical needs. God treats us, as body and soul, holistically. Our physical can have a bearing on our spiritual trials. Elijah had run over eighty plus miles through the hot desert on foot. This was due to the fact that his life was threatened, he had a lot in his mind, it's not unlikely that he was physically and emotionally tired.

Sometimes we feel like what we are going through is too much for us to endure and the truth is, that is correct.

God often calls us to go beyond what we are able to do or endure in order that it will be known He was the one who enabled us to make the hard-impossible journey. By this, we, just like Elijah, see that God is able to get us through anything, no matter how ridiculously hard it is.

In the book of **Deuteronomy 11:17**; The bible says:
Then the LORD's anger will burn against you, and he will shut up the heavens so that it will not rain and the ground will yield no produce, and you will soon perish from the good land the LORD is giving you.   May the Lord help us to understand that when sin enters, He can shut the heavens and releases pestilence to give us a wakeup call, for the wages of sin is death.

In **Daniel 11:32** the scriptures say, those who do wickedly against the covenant he shall corrupt with flattery; but the people who know their God shall be strong, and carry out great exploits.   King Ahab was a principality himself of high level and could not face him anyhow.   Jezebel the witch was a campaigner on how to challenge God of Israel, but who can stand the presence of God.

The bible affirms in **1 Kings 18:1-4 – End,** that, after a long time, in the third year, the word of the LORD came to Elijah: "Go and present yourself to Ahab, and I will send rain on the land." So, Elijah went to present himself to Ahab. Now the famine was severe in Samaria, and Ahab had summoned Obadiah, his palace administrator. Obadiah was a devout believer in the LORD. While Jezebel was killing off the LORD's prophets, Obadiah had taken a hundred prophets and hidden them in two caves, fifty in each, and had supplied them with food and water.

Also, in **1Kings 18:18**, the bible says, when Elijah got to Ahab, he was questioned. "Is that you, you're troubler of Israel?" "I have not made trouble for Israel," Elijah replied. But you and your father's family have. You have abandoned the LORD's commands and have followed the Baals. This was the first encounter. He knew his God can do and so he made a declaration. Today we will know who is the true God. He repaired the destroyed altar. Then Elijah commanded them, "Seize the prophets of Baal. Don't let anyone get away!"

They seized them, and Elijah had them brought down to the Kishon Valley and slaughtered all there **1Kings 18:40**. **Verses 41-46** says, And Elijah said to Ahab, "Go, eat and drink, for there is the sound of a heavy rain." So, Ahab went off to eat and drink, but Elijah climbed to the top of Carmel, bent down to the ground and put his face between his knees. "Go and look toward the sea," he told his servant. And he went up and looked. "There is nothing there," he said. Seven times Elijah said, "Go back."

The seventh time the servant reported, "A cloud as small as a man's hand is rising from the sea." So, Elijah said, "Go and tell Ahab, 'Hitch up your chariot and go down before the rain stops you." Meanwhile, the sky grew black with clouds, the wind rose, a heavy rain started falling and Ahab rode off to Jezreel. The power of the LORD came on Elijah and, tucking his cloak into his belt, he ran ahead of Ahab all the way to Jezreel.

Even though after this encounter his human showed up after he killed the prophets and Jezebel was looking for him so that she could kill him, Elijah ran way. He would have called fire for the king but he knew the law of Moses that touch not my anointed and do my prophet no harm. God would not suffer his faithfulness to fail. When Jesus was on the cross, he almost gave up when he spoke in the flesh, Father remove this cup from me but not my will but your will. God was preparing Elijah for his exit.

Elisha was known by the sons of prophet as one pouring water in the hands of Elijah. He was to be lifted up at some point by all means. The sons of the prophet kept reminding him that his master was about to leave but Elisha kept watching wherever the man of God Elijah went he followed.

God is about to change our destiny. Men looked at our profile and judged us but our name is about to change for good. Keep walking and getting closer to God and clear they thought and be creative and keep your progress. Do not settle for less but act and stop walking with people who have left you and yet you think you are together. They could have looked back but move on for there is hope.

God is about to supernaturally transform you in all areas of your life. Those who kept mocking you will see it for a thousand shall fall on your side and ten thousand on your right and none shall come near your dwelling. All the pain and embarrassment will be overtaken by the breakthrough you will receive in Yeshua's Name.

Think big and shake off your last year or last month dust; for God says, behold I am doing a new thing for He is the beginning and the end. God is about to change the page and everything the enemy has touched; it will be restored a hundred-fold for a new chapter has been opened supernaturally. My reader I pray that you become creative as a genuine believer and you will produce fruit as you endure to the end.

David was a shepherd boy but when Samuel anointed him, he became a king. Before the anointing, lions were killing the sheep but after the anointing he could tear the lion and the bear into pieces with his hands. Fear not for the Lord is on your side beloved. We are in a race not 100 meters not marathon. We need to train hard for it's not given to the swift but more are the battles given to the strong. Rahab was a harlot but she did something for God such that even in the genealogy of Jesus her name is recorded. If your friends quit the race don't quit, but finish the race to the rule and you will receive your reward just like Rahab was supernaturally transformed and so, God is raising our Samuel for we are marked for a destiny.

Samuel anointed David until this triggered jealous in his brothers. The testing of our greatness is hard but when it is perfected, we shine like stars. If you think you are fixed without Christ you are a liar. Don't you be afraid because no demon, no witchcraft can over through the plan of God for your life. He is the only one who can fix you from the mess.

Be in a happening church not a dwarf, for God is interested with relationship not your perfect performance and you are the church. When the anointing is poured upon you and me favour begins to follow us wherever we go. Saul sent for Jesse to send his son David to play harp for him because favour had begun to locate him. You shall be located supernaturally in Yeshua's Mighty Name.

In **1Kings 19:15-18** the bible says After Elijah ran away God showed up and told him wake up and eat for the journey was long. He had to walk for forty days and forty nights until he got to mount Horeb the mountain of God. All he wanted was I have had enough but God wanted him to go and anoint Hazael king over Aram. Also, anoint Jehu son of Nimshi king over Israel, and anoint Elisha son of Shaphat from Abel Meholah to succeed you as prophet. Why are you here? God had not sent him to Horeb as he had to the other places.

Elijah went there out of fear or searching for God to give him answers. God used Elijah's mistake to bring good to him anyway for God is sovereignly God and will take everything in our lives and use it for our good so that we know Him better. God was in a business of preparing Elijah for what was a head of him. Today we fear to open our mouth and tell someone you will be my successor or you will succeed us because of the fear of unknown. So, in our **secret place** that's where we find stamina to pray. Pray again these prayers and you shall overcome for you have already overcome for Jesus (Yeshua) overcame the world for us already and so we should not be afraid for he has our back covered. Please pray these prayers as you read through because God is also preparing you and me for what is ahead of us. We therefore put on the whole armour of God and move on to fight for the battle is not ours but the Lord's

- I pray that anything that want to cripple our lives to burn by fire Yeshua's Name.
- Every spirit of grieve, bankruptcy, failure, famine in our lives be consumed by fire by fire in Yeshua's name.
- I revoke all spells and every satanic pronouncement in our lives in Yeshua's Name.
- Any spirit of harassment against my/your life, my church, my family, and my children be destroyed by fire in Yeshua's Name.

- I terminate any weapon of untimely death against my family, my church, and my children in Yeshua's Name.
- Every false accuser, rumour mongers, be roasted by fire Yeshua's Name.
- Oh! God avenge for me, my church, my family, and my children in Yeshua's Name.
- I secure the harvest of this church, my family, and my children in Yeshua's Name.
- May harmony prevail in my life, in this church, in my family in Yeshua's Name.
- I declare new beginning and release divine provision for my church, my family, my children, my husband, my wife in Yeshua's Name.
- Oh Lord catapults me into greatness as you did for Daniel, in the land of Babylon Yeshua's Name.
- I reject slippery blessings in Yeshua's Name.
- Any satanic influence that has stopped my name from being remembered is destroyed in Yeshua's Name.

- Any evil meeting summoned against my promotion scatter by thunder and earthquake in Yeshua's Name.

- Oh Lord may my enemies and their stronghold be shattered to pieces by thunder of God in Yeshua's Name.

- Any evil charm or sacrifice buried because of me, my church, my family, and children is exhumed by earthquake in Yeshua's Name.

- Every collective captivity receives fire and divine axe in Yeshua's Name.

- Any foundational serpent and scorpion, programmed into my life to destroy my calling in the future die by fire in Yeshua's Mighty Name.

- I challenge by fire every thrown challenging my enthronement through the bond of collective captivity, catch the fire of God in Yeshua's Name.

- Every witchcraft programme drawn through collective captivity for my family, my church, be overthrown by fire Yeshua's Name.

- Father God disgrace every power that is out to steal our program for our life in the name of Yeshua's Name.
- Today we receive angelic transportation to where God wants us to be in Yeshua's Name.
- It does not matter whether I deserves it or not, I receives unquantifiable favour from the Lord like Isaac in Yeshua's Name.
- Let God who answers by fire spit fire into my situation today and wipe out failure and defeat in Yeshua's Name.
- Let every spiritual cobweb spread over any of my documents be roasted by fire in Yeshua's Name.
- May the glory of my calling arise and shine in the name of Yeshua.
- I refuse to retire; I must rekindle the fire of God in me in Yeshua's Mighty Name.
- I receive power to meet the needs of this present generation in Yeshua's mighty Name.
- Strength of God empower me and all my readers In Yeshua's Mighty Name.

May the Lord give us a supernatural breakthrough in our mind because we have the mind of Christ to say No! No! to the devil.

No one can save your character, nor safe your integrity. Even the cure for aids HIV is not condoms and the gospel of safe sex, but the solution is the God given power to say No to it. No one will help us to start living at our reach but not on borrowed clothes, cars, jewels and even food.

Know that our enemy the devil is an oppressor and can frighten us, and this can even make a believer to become half-hearted in their faith. Oppression of every kind can remove your alertness, as the devil makes it too big and he puts a magnifying glass on you when the spirit of fear comes in but we pray and destroy all in Yeshua's Name. Just say no to the devil and use the little that you have, if possible, to proclaim the gospel for the Master is coming soon. All the rest of material possessions are vanity of vanity. May the Lord multiply grace upon your life and anointing of revelation which will permanently change your history in Yeshua's Mighty Name.

## CHAPTER SEVEN

## SPEAKING TO DRY BONES IN YOUR SECRET PLACE.

We need to know that since we are heirs and not beggars of the Kingdom of God, we ought to speak to every area of our lives, as we trust God to do what He has promised and He will transform us supernaturally in this very dispensation era.

**Ezekiel 37:7** affirms the word of God saying, So, I prophesied as I was commanded; and as I prophesied, there was a noise, and behold, a rattling; and the bones came together, bone to its bone. As many more people seem to be talking about an all-encompassing UNITY among all religions and all denominations, it is imperative that we see how True Unity really works and what are we to expect from it.

In the book of Ezekiel, we encounter a chapter that carries the secret of true unity and its FRUIT! First of all, Chapter 37 was written about the End Time Restoration of Israel but its illustration can be used for the Church as well. Ezekiel finds himself in the midst of a valley full of bones that represent the scattered People of Israel in the nations. It is obvious from the passage that while they are scattered and disjointed there is no hope for them. The only hopes lie in the UNITING of these scattered and dry bones.

Indeed, this has been happening for nearly 70 years since the liberation of Auschwitz. Jews from all over the world have come back home and have become a nation again! Indeed the "skeletons" rescued from the Nazi Death Camps joined together bone to its bone, were infused with a New Spirit and have become a Mighty Army that has survived every wicked war launched against her by her Arab-Muslim neighbours!

The work of redemption is not yet finished of course saints, since many more "bones" need to join this Mighty Army of Jews in the Land of Israel, such as the Anusim that lost their Jewish identity due to the Spanish Inquisition, the Sephardic or Spanish Jews. However, Ezekiel 37 has been unfolding before the eyes of the entire world.

In the same manner we can relate to the need of true unity in the body of Messiah as an in gathering of dry bones that came together "bone to its bone". And what does that mean? It means that there is a Divine Order of Unity, just like not all the bones fit in the same way in our physical bodies, so in the Body of Messiah not all bones go together. Rather each bone needs to be fitting in ITS PROPER PLACE. This will be supernaturally done by the Almighty God. The reason for so much disorder, is pain and powerlessness are because people are trying to form a "manmade unity" that is not divinely ordained.

There are bones that belong together to form a certain member in the Body but they are apart. There are others that need to be apart or joining with other bones but they have formed wrong alliances and are trying to bring unity their way. Bones need to fit in ORDER, order of leadership, Five-Fold ministry and the rest of the Saints according to their gifting and Divine Placement.

**Ephesians 4:10-12** say He who descended is Himself also He who ascended far above all the heavens, so that He might fill all things. And He gave some as apostles, and some as prophets, and some as evangelists, and some as pastors and teachers, for the equipping of the saints for the work of service, to the building up of the body of Messiah. We must surrender to YHVH as a simple soldier that is placed by his/her Commander in the proper Army Unit according to the proper rank. It is not where I want to be but where do YOU want me Lord to be. It is not who I want to be with but who the Lord want me to join with. It is not who I want to be but rather knowing called me to be for he is Adonai

It has nothing to do with our logic, likes or dislikes but rather divine placement. This can only be achieved through the power of prayer in our secret places. Until the bones fit in their exact Divine Placement and are faithful to serve there as a Joint that supplies, there are three things that will not happen.

- There will be no wholeness (no sinews or ligaments).
- The Spirit will not come or this is to say revival will not happen.

- We will not become a Mighty Army and so, what we need to do should be our question.

Saints, we need to pray with UNDERSTANDING and COURAGE. May your home become a place of prayer in all seasons. Pray without ceasing until the power of God is manifest in your life my reader. Like Jesus wept over Jerusalem let your prayers come from your heart making sure you are seeking God with self-seeking goals to get the agenda of God. We can minister the word to ourselves and other and get to a place of believing God that prayer changes things. Make time to speak to the dry bones in your and my jurisdiction in Yeshua's Mighty Name.

Father in Heaven forgive us for trying to make unity happen in the flesh and for placing ourselves where we see fit. May we surrender to your order and placement in our life. Please dismantle any unholy alliances in our life and throughout the Body of Messiah. Now Lord I ask you to bring bone to its bone and to fit those people that are to be together in my life, in our ministry or congregation and in the Body of Messiah at large in Jesus name.

We command the right bones to come together and to be Divinely fitted forming a Healthy Body that You El Shaddai can fill with Your Spirit and empower to become Your Mighty End Time Army to reach this generation with the Gospel of the Kingdom in Yeshua's Name.

If you prayed that prayer for yourself, your Ministry and the Body at large, expect it to be answered in many surprising ways and be humble to let YHVH do the fitting and bring in the True Unity. Accept the place that He gives you, no more, no less. This can happen in the Macro Level (The Body of Messiah at large) and in the Micro Level, the Congregation or Ministry you belong to and even your personal circle of family and friends.

One of the reasons why is the Body of Messiah is in Skeletal Disorder with bones trying to fit in the wrong places is the estrangement from the original Apostolic Foundations of the Faith which are Jewish. The restoration of the Biblical Apostolic Hebrew Foundations which is a catalyst of Divine order which leads to Divine Empowerment of the Body of Messiah at large.

Only prayers can help us to take stock of our lives and avoid wrong theologies but rise up in new power for it's time for new release of power. We are the house of prayer for the Spirit of God lives in church and as the church arise bones will attach to themselves and in perfect order.

The book of **Romans 11:18** tells us not be arrogant toward the (Jewish) branches, but if you are arrogant, remember that it is not you who supports the root, but the root supports you. The dragon of old knows it and he has tried every trick he has and evil weapon in order to stop the End Time Messianic-Apostolic-Prophetic Movement! So, the dragon was enraged with the woman (Israel), and went off to make war with the rest of her children, who keep the commandments of God and those who hold to the testimony of Yeshua according to **Revelation 12:17**.

But praise be to God prayed His prayer in **John 17** that will not remain unanswered! It will soon manifest together with the Most Powerful Revival the world has ever seen. So, I prophesied as He commanded me, and the breath came into them, and they came to life and stood on their feet, an exceedingly great army. **Ezekiel 37:10**

So, today the Lord would want us to command the earth to vomit back that which belongs to us that it had swallowed. The empty prayers we have been praying are replaced by the effectual fervent prayer of a righteous which availed much as we read in the book of **James 5:16b**. Let's have an intimate relationship with God in our secret place. It's only the anointing that breaks the yoke. Let's become a house of prayer and this is how God will be able to hear and answer us. It's not our way but God's way but bones will receive new fresh in Jesus Mighty Name.

The earth has ears according to **Jeremiah 22:29** which says, O earth, earth, earth, hear the word of the LORD.
I mentioned this again but I must emphasis the earth hears. This season, our seed must yield its fruit 100%. It's a season when God is bringing out His very own children and declaring them publicly that they belong to Him. I declare today according to the word of God, that the Lord shall perfect everything concerning us and He who started the

good works in us will complete it **(Philippian 1:6)**. Every bone must go back to its place without further delay in Jesus Name.

As we start to please God nothing will be above the agenda of God. Not our wives, not our children, not our money, not even our positions will be a hinderance. We will put all these behind us and go back to God for the altars to burn with the presence of God. We put away our angry and childish games and God will answer the cry of His people and establish his house which will be called a house of prayer for the nations. Avoid those cheap and ceiling prayers but pray from your heart believing God who is the only one who can make us go through any dry season in our lives. He will help us to call those things that are not as though they are or into being.

Help us to turn into the first love so that the fire in our hearts, your churches and families will be rekindled and help us to stop the spirit of procrastination, so we may call you and as you have promised you will hear us.

We lender our hearts and not our garments for you are a covenant keeping God and help us God and forgive us and redeem us so that the love of Jesus Christ will come back and none will be found with the itching ears. We lay the axe of prayer to the root of wicked tree and silence every spirit of Peninnah, every enchantment or divination in Yeshua's Name.

**Psalms 92:7. Says,** "That when the wicked sprouted up like grass and all who did iniquity flourished, it was only that they might be destroyed forevermore." Supernaturally, the Lord will snatch his own from the jaws of the enemy. We refuse to allow the enemy to make incantation or any invocation against us, let fire rain down and consume them in Yeshua's Name.

The book of **Ecclesiastes 8:11** says, Because the sentence against an evil deed is not executed quickly, therefore the hearts of the sons of men among them are given fully to do evil. May the Lord Execute judgement to every evil doer who has stood against our progress, our children, our ministry, our finance, and implement judgement speedily in Yeshua's Mighty Name.

God can give us ability to create wealth or wealth created by others. He can strengthen us to conquer or weaken our enemies. We need to know that there are things that we must conquer and make sure we do. We must suppress our body if we want to receive life that God has promised those who will become the righteousness of God because they have overcome the flesh and its desire, such as; Selfishness, un forgiveness, unbelieve, idolatry, fornication, adultery etc.

For bones to come to their place these must be conquered, not by might neither power but by the blood of Jesus. I realise that there is need for the outpouring of our spirit so that we may redeem and restore all what the enemy has stollen from the church in the Mighty Name of Yeshua (Jesus Christ). We are the church and so work out until you and I win for we are winners. So, lets pray the following prayers as we read through this book.

We shall send confusion into the camp of every demonic agents. God made Moses a god over pharaoh in **Exodus 7;1** so, we shall send the task master parking and disgrace pharaoh and all his horsemen. Every enemy that will not let you go to connect with your bone and the perfect will of God will be disgraced and killed as we command them to release every believer in Yeshua's Mighty Name. Every satanic decision taken against the progress of the church we nullify by the power of God. Even as we pray the following prayers by faith.

- **Every good door the enemy has shut for us, I command it to open now by their own accord in Yeshua's Mighty Name.**
- **I now speak with a holy anger that every siege (barrier) in my life scatter by fire in Yeshua's Mighty Name.**
- **Any witch pointing a finger at us that we will come back empty we judge them by fire and let their finger wither in Yeshua's Mighty Name.**
- **Every evil arrow or spell targeted to us we send it back to sender.**

- Every scud missile thrown to us we send them back to sender in Yeshua's Mighty Name.

- Every evil remote control being used to manipulate my pregnancy roast by fire in Yeshua's Mighty Name.

- May every demonic authority in this vicinity be crippled and silenced in Yeshua's Mighty Name.

- Every power working against us, our prosperity, children, husbands, ministries fall down and die in Yeshua's Mighty Name.

- Mercy has been released to us for we have connected bone to bone, tendon to tendon in Yeshua's Mighty Name.

## CHAPTER EIGHT

## BREAKING BARRIERS

The bible says in **1Kings 2:1-4**;

Now the days of David drew nigh that he should die and he charged Solomon his son, saying, I go the way of all the earth, be thou strong therefore, and shew thyself a man; And keep the charge of the LORD thy God, to walk in his ways, to keep his statutes, and his commandments, and his judgments, and his testimonies, as it is written in the law of Moses, that thou mayest prosper in all that thou does, and whithersoever thou turnest thyself.  That the LORD may continue his word which he spoke concerning me, saying, If thy children take heed to their way, to walk before me in truth with all their heart and with all their soul, there shall not fail thee (said he) a man on the throne of Israel.

Similarly, in **Exodus 8,** the scriptures say, Then the LORD said to Moses, Go to Pharaoh and say to him, 'This is what the LORD says, let my people go, so that they may worship me.

If you refuse to let them go, I will send a plague of frogs on your whole country. The Nile will teem with frogs. They will come up into your palace and your bedroom and onto your bed, into the houses of your officials and on your people, and into your ovens and kneading troughs.

The frogs will come up on you and your people and all your officials." I declare and decree, any Pharaoh barriers to be broken from your lives my readers in Yeshua's Name. let go those people whom you are holding. Set them free and you will be free as well.

The bible says in **Acts 3:1-10** that, one day Peter and John were going up to the temple at the time of prayer at three in the afternoon. Now a man who was lame from birth was being carried to the temple gate called Beautiful, where he was put every day to beg from those going into the temple courts. When he saw Peter and John about to enter, he asked them for money. Peter looked straight at him, as did John. Then Peter said, "Look at us!" and so, the man gave them his attention, expecting to get something from them.

Then Peter said, Silver or gold I do not have, but what I do have I give you. In the name of Jesus Christ of Nazareth, walk. Taking him by the right hand, he helped him up, and instantly the man's feet and ankles became strong. He jumped to his feet and began to walk.

Then he went with them into the temple courts, walking and jumping, and praising God. When all the people saw him walking and praising God, they recognized him as the same man who used to sit begging at the temple gate called Beautiful, and they were filled with wonder and amazement at what had happened to him.

My reader every barrier and limitation must be broken and we are going to look at how Barriers are created and where they come from. In the book of **1 Corinthians 16:9** the bible says, for there is a great door for effective work has opened to me, and there are many who oppose me. Yes, my reader, you may have a perpetual door open but there are many adversaries to conquer in your, marriages, among your children, even in your business, in your jobs, in your families. Remember God is well able to supernaturally transform all these areas in His might.

Also, **Zachariah 13:6** tells us if someone asks, 'What are these wounds on your body?' they will answer, 'The wounds I was given at the house of my friends.' Zachariah sustained wounds from his friend and this is to remind us that we get hurt by our own. The very people who should protect you could be your betrayals if not killers. Moreover, **Jeremiah 5:26** says, among my people are wicked men who lie in wait for victims like a hunter hiding in a blind. They continually set traps to catch people. Racheal would have married seven years earlier if there was no Leah in her life according to **Genesis 29:18-21**.

Your trouble is in your own house. With Haman alive Mordechai would have remained at the gate. Your enemies must die in your place in Yeshua's Name. Change your past and arise. Change your status quo and do uncommon for uncommon miracles. Mordechai told Ester you are in Palace for such a time as this.

Locate your prophet for the walls to fall down. Remember you cannot attract what you do not place value on. **Hebrews 11:23** also says Moses was hidden for three months and so every hidden blessing will be excavated out. This can only be done by the power of God's authority that you must speak it out.

Likewise, in the book of **Joshua 9:27** the bible says, that day he made the Gibeonites woodcutters and water carriers for the assembly, to provide for the needs of the altar of the LORD at the place the LORD would choose. And that is what they are to this day. Brethren, let us train our people and make them engineers and they will be even in the days to come.

In conclusion of this chapter please allow me to say to us what the scriptures has made me to know in the book of **Rev 16:13**, which says, Then I saw three impure spirits that looked like frogs; they came out of the mouth of the dragon, out of the mouth of the beast and out of the mouth of the false prophet. Brothers and sisters, saints of God be careful of the false prophets.

Church arise it's about time and the sound of the trumpet is near and I repeat myself, it will not be long. Get yourself ready for the groom is coming only for the bride who has prepared herself in her **secret place**.

## Isaiah 60: 3, 6, 8,13

- "Arise, shine, for your light has come, and the glory of the LORD rises upon you.
- Herds of camels will cover your land, young camels of Midian and Ephah.
- And all from Sheba will come, bearing gold and incense and proclaiming the praise of the LORD.
- "Who are these that fly along like clouds, like doves to their nests? The glory of Lebanon will come to you, the juniper, the fir and the cypress together, to adorn my sanctuary; and I will glorify the place for my feet.

Cross over your barriers for the enemy to embrace you as the Lord sets a table for you right before them.

Then you and I will know that "When famous speak industrious keep quiet." My reader the Lord has spoken.

This is why Jesse would have created a barrier for David because he was using his physical eyes. The Lord had to supernaturally transform David even though he was smelling like sheep.

His father thought the mighty sons he had were to be anointed the king but God does not look at the outward appearance but always goes and sees in the secret place. God had recognised David while he was tendering the sheep. He will recognise us today wherever we are in Yeshua's Name. As you are reading this book today believe with your heart that God has locate you and God Himself will perfect all that concerns you.

The bible says in **Joshua 6:25**, But Joshua spared Rahab the prostitute, with her family and all who belonged to her, because she hid the men Joshua had sent as spies to Jericho and she lives among the Israelites to this day. Rahab would have created a barrier for the spies, but she protected them. She and her family were protected from the wrath. Her secret became her destiny.

Joshua spared Rahab for hiding the spies and this means whatever you are hiding today can become your life tomorrow. Hide the Holy Spirit in your heart and he will transform you in all your endeavour. Achan and his family were destroyed for hiding that which was not holy before God and so they became a stumbling block. Host God in your secret place and never hind sin for it will kill you.

The bible says that the wages of sin is death. **Joshua 7:19-21** says, Then Joshua said to Achan, my son, tell the truth. Confess to the LORD, the God of Israel. Tell me what you did, and don't try to hide anything from me. Achan answered, "It is true! I have sinned against the LORD, the God of Israel. This is what I did, Among the things I saw was a beautiful coat from Babylonia and about five pounds of silver and more than one and one-fourth pounds of gold.

I wanted these things very much for myself, so I took them. You will find them buried in the ground under my tent, with the silver underneath."

Be careful on what you are hiding, it can bring death or life to you and your household. Whatever sin we hind, it's only from man but God knows it all. One man made so many Israelites to be killed and Joshua had to cry to God until He revealed to him that there was sin in the camp. Sometimes believers go through so much because they probably have entered into a covenant but they are not confessing.

People go through so much asking everybody everywhere to pray for them but no change. Until you go back to your drawing board and check what you are hiding and exhume it for your deliverance. Achan hid what he thought was good for him but it brought destruction to him and his household. God is not mocked and you cannot lie to him, neither can you lie to the devil and even to yourself. My reader kill whatever it is you are hiding before it destroys you and it before it kills you everything around you.

## CHAPTER NINE

## ENVIRONMENT AND CHRISTIANS

At this end times I have considered to say something in this chapter about our environment as a people called of God to be His voice and representative in this galaxy, we need even in our secret place to reconsider this topic, the environment and Christians.

In my view everyone should now have a take in how natural systems are managed and elements of nature. This is to say change must begin from within and so environmental issues must be developed by all and appropriate moral basis followed. God created and so will sustain all element and systems in his creation.

In **Genesis 1:1-25,** the earth, sky and all-natural elements formed such as minerals water, rocks air vegetation, water animals and wildlife are all the environment. So, in the beginning God created the heavens and the earth. He then created Adam the first man and put him in the garden of

Eden to look after it. He instructed him to watch over it and wisely make use of it. A righteous man cares for the need of his animals and **proverbs 12:10** is a good reference. We human beings should take care of the environment and our souls as a matter of fact.

**Genesis 1:28** establishes that in God's basic ordering of Creation, people have dominion over nature. However, it also clearly states the people are creations of God. As creations of God, people are under the authority or dominion of God. Hence, from the viewpoint of God's authority and control, people and nature are in the same order and all creation as well as people must submit to God's plans and ways.

According to **Revelation 4:11** you are worthy to receive all the glory, honour and power for all you created and by your will they were all created and have their being. Do not forget despite the fact that he gave us dominion, the earth is his and everything in it and all who live in it **Psalms 24:1**. So, man is without excuses to respect environment because God loves and enjoys it.

Heaven declares his glory; skies proclaim the work of his hands day and night they display his knowledge according to the book of **Psalms 19:1-4**. God has given dominion to man over nature and has kept its functioning to provide life and support for each other.

Sin has separated man with God and people from themselves and nature. For all have sinned and fallen short of God's glory according to **Romans 2:23**. Instead of man knowing that creation waits in eager expectation for the sons of God to be revealed. This is to say physical environment is not destined for external destruction.

There will be new heaven and new earth, new physical bodies and new physical beginning for the natural world and universe.

In **Genesis 9,** God established covenant with Noah, his sons, descendants and every living creature that was with him. This in other words is to say we must establish Christian environmental ethics and stewardship.

We must take care for the environment. The earth belongs to God and we are stewards. Since the earth is the Lords humanity has a responsibility to serve and keep God creation. Humanity should exercise dominion without destroying environment but to serve it and keep its environmentalist. These things will only be revealed in our **secret place** when we have intimacy with God.

Furthermore, I believe environment problems are more spiritual than technological. We should therefore study what creation reveals, the creator and stewardship of His world. Christians should become committed to the recycling possibly to reduce carbon from our environment. There is little hope of resolution in a short term, due to recession, indifferences, political divisions which keeps getting in the way. So, the full integration of human's society and nature, into the vision of the peace that God intended. As the children of God these are facts that we must know.

If we human being understand the need of taking care of the environment then all the microplastics through aquatic life that ends up in the oceans should stop and not continue, otherwise, there will be more plastic bottles in the oceans than fish in a few years' time. However, if we can stretch ourselves theologically and philosophically, we could understand why God created human beings in his image.

We are also interrelated with non-human creatures whom we share this environment on earth together. If we all take responsibilities by segregating and cleaning up, reusing recycling and managing waste including plastics wherever we are but if possible, we should avoid all plastics. The Bible explains that when we put our faith and trust in God, He will lead us to an eternal heavenly home which he has prepared for us. It's our duty to put everything within our reach, in order to please God.

Nonetheless, until he calls us to live forever with him in our heavenly homes, we will have to live in the physical homes which He has provided for us. This is to say our physical homes includes the whole planet earth, the numerous natural environments found on this planet called the earth, our townships and capitals, and the houses or flats where we live and sleep. If all this is calm then we can easily hear God in our secret place.

God desired that human beings should flourish through with desire for all creation to flourish. Human have a guest for immortality hence the ant aging technology. So, Christians should think on environmental need with deeper understanding of humanity relationship with nature as it is lived out in society and in communities. Subsequently, the key to addressing environmental and social problem is the intersection of non-reducibility of morality and social structures and earth. This is to say when the fear of the Lord becomes our priority then we will make a difference in all areas.

When a precise natural resource or environmental subject or problem arises, people and groups in most cases disagree on the suitable course of action to resolve the issues in question. At the core of these differences, there are different values and beliefs associated to nature itself, the use and management of nature. The system of values and beliefs that encourages how an individual's thinks and acts is known as that person's ethical system. There is no scripture that supports the belief of some of the Christians in the modern church who think nature does not matter since it's part of the physical world.

The bible says, for since the creation of the world God's invisible qualities his eternal power and divine nature have been clearly seen, being understood from what has been made, so that people are without excuse.

For although they knew God, they neither glorified him as God nor gave thanks to him, but their thinking became futile and their foolish hearts were darkened. Although they claimed to be wise, they became fools and exchanged the glory of the immortal God for images made to look like a mortal human being and birds and animals and reptiles, according to the book of **Romans 1:20 – 23**.

This passage is referring to those who know God but raised nature to be objects or idols of worship. The worship of whatsoever in nature changes the order of the Second Commandment in which God stated: "You shall not make for yourself an idol in the form of anything in heaven above or on the earth beneath or in the waters below.

You shall not bow down to them or worship them" as stated in **Exodus 20:4-5, NIV.**

One of the main reasons God created and continues to sustain nature, as mentioned earlier is for God himself to love and enjoy. Another reason is to be able to meet the needs of his people whom he created, such as food and shelter, backed by **Genesis 2:15; Genesis 9:3.** Another major purpose of nature is to glorify and reveal God to his people universally, which we can refer to is **Psalm 19:1-4 and Romans 1:18-20.** For example, **Psalm 19:14** states: The heavens declare the glory of God; the skies proclaim the work of his hands. Day after day they pour forth speech; night after night they display knowledge.

There is no speech or language where their voice is not heard. Their voice goes out into all the earth, their words to the ends of the world **Psalm 19:14, NIV.** For God to meet his intended purpose of his creation he sustains all of creation within particular orders. The first large-scale Creation ordering of interest is the Biblical hierarchy between God, nature and people. Understanding and applying a Christian environmental ethic requires a proper interpretation of Biblical verses establishing and describing this basic hierarchy. The earth is a planet with different environments such as forests, deserts, oceans, lakes and rivers which God created with natural life-support systems in his mind and design.

God made numerous major chemical cycles into our home called the earth. God is the architecture and the builder and all of these cycles aids to provide what is needed to support life on earth. One example, the carbon and oxygen cycle help in providing breathable air and normalise global temperatures at a level that helps us to live. The hydrologic cycle helps to provide water that we drink and for many other purposes. This was all in God's plan before He began to speak let there be.

All the different chemical cycles that we see or know contributes to the provision of mineral resources such as oil, coal, electricity, natural gas that we use as fuel for transportation, and heating.

These cycles also support renewable resources such as trees and fish and wildlife. We use trees for consumptive uses such as lumber, and to support non-consumptive uses such as recreation and artistic enjoyment. We use fish and wildlife for consumptive uses such as harvesting ocean fish for food, and hunting of wildlife on public and private lands. We also use fish and wildlife for non-consumptive frivolous uses and aesthetic enjoyment such as wildlife observation and photography according to (Barrett and Bergstrom).

When people use elements of nature for commercial production and consumption, and even recreational and aesthetic enjoyment, some level of waste-by products enter the environment. Smoke stakes into the air and effluent discharge pipes into rivers which are obvious evidence of these waste by-products. When people use a forest or park for recreation, waste by-products are emitted into the air from automobiles, and motorboats and so on. Solid wastes in the form of litter are also often left behind as stated by (John C. Bergstrom).

God made waste integration and treatment abilities into natural systems. For example, scientists have recognised the natural talent of wetlands to filter chemicals out of water that are potentially harmful to human health. However, extreme use of a specific natural system such as a wetland area by people for waste by-product clearance may threaten the continued ability of that natural system to conform and treat wastes.

The God given role of people as caretakers or managers of elements of nature and natural systems is illustrated through several linkages. People manage nature, for example, by cultivating the land to grow and harvest crops for food through agriculture, and to grow and harvest trees for wood products through forestry. God gave man dominion over all things that he made before he went astray when he sinned against God. **Genesis 1:28** the bible says God blessed them and said to them, be fruitful and increase in number; fill the earth and subdue it. Rule over the fish in the sea and the birds in the sky and over every living creature that moves on the ground.

Nevertheless, God's people, manages lakes, and rivers, to produce energy, to provide drinking water besides supporting different types of recreational events, such as boating and swimming. They also involve themselves in managing ecosystems to provide fish and wildlife habitation and other broad environmental facilities such as protection of regional air and water quality, or even regulation of global climate.

God's people manage nature through waste and pollution management and policy. Such as, they design and build waste treatment facilities to filter harmful materials out of human sewage waste water before the water is discharged into the environment.

They also design and implement best management practices for reducing all the waste runoff from construction sites, farms, and forest and mining operations. Scholars in the humanities, social sciences and physical and biological sciences have accentuated that environmental issues and problems are fundamentally interrelated with ethical issues and problems. Do not forget God promised he will release wisdom to his people.

Consequently, we are hearing more voices saying that in order to resolve environmental issues and problems, people need to advance and follow an appropriate moral basis for dealing with the environment. This distinguishes a basic inhabitant of human behaviour taught in the Bible. That, true change starts from within a person's heart, mind and spirit and works outward as reflected by attitudes and actions. This can be backed by **Luke 6:45**, which says a good man brings good things out of the good stored up in his heart, and an evil man brings evil things out of the evil stored up in his heart. For the mouth speaks what the heart is full of.

Therefore, in all areas of our lives, the substance of our inner faith determines the living out or practice of our faith. Additionally, others are trained and hired to advance and enforce policies and laws for or to be regulating the discharge or emissions of waste by-products into the environment from a variety of sources including point sources (for example manufacturing plants) and nonpoint sources (e.g., automobiles). Yet still, God assumes his creation will give back to nature since it was his intended purposes for his creation to act in a responsible manner and be caretakers of nature. The Bible teaches that God loves and enjoys all that He has created. The Psalmist, states in **Psalms 145:16-17,** you open your hand and satisfy the desires of every living thing. No wonder he created man in his own image and if you seek him from your **secret place**, He will give you an open heaven for he created man with the mind of Christ.

The LORD is righteous in all his ways and faithful in all he does. Thus, an important implication of the Principle of Creation value from an ethical perspective is that God places value on elements of the environment independent of human use and human-centred values as **Genesis 1:25** says, God made the wild animals according to their kinds, the livestock according to their kinds, and all the creatures that move along the ground according to their kinds. And God saw that it was good.

If God's creation becomes poor stewards especially in agriculture, they farm a tract of land until the soil is totally burned out and it becomes incapable for any further production. Over harvesting in the forests and mishandling a forest such that new trees can no longer be grown is poor stewardship.

Also, if there is exceeding the capacity of air and water resources to absorb and disperse pollution so that air and water become unsafe to consume is an example of poor stewardship in the environmental pollution management area. God want us to be faithful with what he has entrusted in our hands.

The other extreme position on the value and importance of the physical world and nature that Christians should not fall into is one that improperly elevates the status of nature to being equal to or even above people. The Scripture teaches that although God values nature, he places a special higher value on people who he crowned with glory and honour as the climax of his creation in **Genesis 1:26-30** and also **Psalms 8:5-8** which says, you have made them a little lower than the angels and crowned them with glory and honour. You made them rulers over the works of your hands, you put everything under their feet, all flocks and herds, and the animals of the wild, the birds in the sky, and the fish in the sea, all that swim the paths of the seas.

The Christian environmental steward must always understand that the elements of nature or natural systems that one is involved in, using or managing are ultimately controlled by God according to His ways and plans. Whether one is involved in the use and management of forestland, farmland, parks, air, natural areas, and water resources at a large-scale, the Christian environmental steward apprehends that human use and management of nature which run counter to God's ways and plans are harmful to nature and eventually to his creation. There is also an awareness that whenever we go our own way rather than following God, He is saddened by our actions.

To be able to carry out responsibilities, the Christian environmental steward tries to learn as much as he or she can about the God-intended order and purpose of nature. This effort includes learning about individual elements of nature, and how these elements of nature function within natural systems created and sustained by God.

The triune God continues to hold together or sustain the functioning of nature, accomplishing his intended order and purpose for all non-living and living elements of the environment and environmental systems. I believe what God is saying is that the Christian environmental steward must put this knowledge into practice by doing their best to use and manage nature within the boundaries of God's ways and plans. Let us not lie to ourselves, for God is not mocked.

## CHAPTER TEN

## WHERE HAVE YOU SETTLED?

**Genesis 20:1-3**, the bible makes it clear and says, And Abraham journeyed from there toward the south country, and dwelled between Kadesh and Shur, and sojourned in Gerar. And Abraham said of Sarah his wife, she is my sister and Abimelech king of Gerar sent, and took Sarah. But God came to Abimelech in a dream by night, and said to him, behold; you are but a dead man, for the woman which you have taken; for she is a man's wife. Remember they will hate you in all towns for the sake of the gospel, but if they hate you in one town move to the next. My brothers and sisters don't settle where you are not accepted but rather keep digging.

**Genesis 26:18** tells us that, and Isaac departed there, and pitched his tent in the valley of Gerar, and dwelled there. Isaac reopened the wells that had been dug in the time of his father Abraham, which the Philistines had stopped up after Abraham died, and he gave them the same names his father had given them.   Before this Isaac had gone to Abimelech king of the Philistines in Gerar.   At this time the Lord appeared to Isaac and told him not to move from Egypt even though there was famine.   The people of the land asked him about his wife and he said she was his sister since Rebekah was so beautiful and he feared the men there might kill him.   Remember when Abraham also said Sarah was his sister.   I trust that you have gleaned something my reader as you keep reading this book.

**Vs 16** say, Isaac became so wealth and the King ordered him to move away from them.   He moved and settled at a valley called Gerar.   The people said the water was theirs and so he called the well Esek because they disputed with him.   Stop arguing for things that are not yours.   God is God of set up.   Joseph's brother had to destroy the coat of many colours his father had made for him, but they never killed his vision.   God had to set it up for him to be sold so that he will rescue them at some point.

Isaac knew they have taken the well but not his vision. Kept digging. Then they dug another well and the people disputed and he called it **Sitnah meaning confusion.**

Isaac then moved on and dug another well and no one quarrelled over it. He named it Rehoboth meaning now the Lord has given us room and we will flourish in the land. Never be content for God is in the business of setting up matters. And may your vision expand in Jesus name. In the secret place Isaac knew how to wait and not argue, but kept pursuing his vision. You may have fallen for the second time but God is in the business so, keep digging. Many are the affliction of the righteous but God shall deliver them from all according to **Psalms 34:19**.

My reader, receive the goodness of the Lord in the land of the living in Yeshua (Jesus name). Oh Lord as Abraham received Favour from you let my reader also receive your favour so that he/she can excel in the name of Jesus. Lord help my readers to refuse to give the accuser of brethren any legal ground in their life and desire to keep digging in

Yeshua's Name. As you remain focused the Lord will settle you in your Rehoboth for his promises are yes and amen.

My reader shall not backslide because people have taken their well. Holy Spirit let not work of darkness thrive in their life. May they keep jumping and walking until they reach their Rehoboth. Never allow anyone to stop you from digging because they have taken the well. Go to the next city and dig another one brothers and sisters and God will give you the grace to endure. If they fight you because of Ministry, don't give up, for He who called you is faithful to the end.

For your information, the well am talking about this the same well where Jesus was met by the Samaritan woman who had married for five times (the number of grace) and yet she was not content until she met the sixth man who changed her destiny forever. This woman had the blood of a Jew and a Samaritan. God understands the jigsaw my dear friends. He already knew you before you were conceived and so He has a good plan for you.

Before we were all knitted in our mother's womb God had already known our ending before the beginning.

Isaac then went to Beersheba and that night the Lord appeared to him and told him I will bless you and increase the number of your descendants for the sake of my servant Abraham. Isaac built an altar there and called on the name of the Lord. There he pitched his tent and there his servants dug a well. Abimelech and his advisor followed him because the blessings of the Lord had located him. Isaac asked them why they have followed him since he chased him away.

Abimelech told him because we now have known the Lord is with you, we would like to make a treaty that you will not harm us. Isaac made a feast for them and next early morning the men swore an oath to each other. May the Lord make your enemy to be a peace with you. I declare that a covenant will be established between you and your pursuers for staying connected in your secret place and also may God's favour locate you in Yeshua's Mighty Name.

That day Isaac servant dug a well and he called it Shibah and to this day the name of the town is Beersheba. Today may you receive angelic transportation to where God wants you to be now in the name of Jesus Christ. Oh Lord, God of Abraham, Isaac and Jacob, catapult my reader into greatness as you did for Daniel in the land of Babylon.

I reject slippery blessings on your behalf in the name of Jesus Christ our Lord and Saviour. Lord may you please scatter the enemies of progress and their stronghold be shattered to pieces by thunder of God in my readers life in Yeshua's Hamashiach Name. See the love of God to us remains overwhelming and we should hold unto the astonishing word of God to demonstrate the magnitude power of His love and care for us.

Yeshua (Jesus Christ) is the only one who can fix you from the mess. When the anointing is poured upon us favour begins to follow us wherever we go.

God is about to change the page and everything the enemy has touched will be restored a hundred-fold for a new chapter has been opened. Remember not the former things my reader but stretch your vision. Habakkuk wrote the vision; Abraham was told to look up and count the stars. May God help you to set your spiritual goals in Yeshua Mighty Name.

Isaac set his goals and he kept digging until he settled at Rehoboth as the Lord had given him room to prosper. May we prosper in Jesus name! It's imperious that the word of God becomes predominant in our life affairs brethren in order to have what we did not have, before we have to do, what we have not done before. The bible says in **Jeremiah 20:11,** therefore, the mighty awesome God is with us and all our persecutors will stumble and not prevail in Jesus Christ Mighty Name. They will greatly be ashamed for they will not prosper and their everlasting confusion will never be forgotten.

Remember the crucifixion of our Lord and Saviour Jesus Christ. I compare it with Isaac the son of the promise to Abraham. Isaac carried the wood up to the mountain that he would be sacrificed.

He participated willingly with what the father was about to do. Jesus willingly laid down his life. He carried his wood ragged cross to the mountain (Golgotha) where He was to be sacrificed. He submitted to the will of His father but he eventually conjured the last enemy to mankind which is death. It was God's will to crush him and make his life an offering for sin. To God be the glory saints we were redeemed from the curse for who knew no sin became sin for our sake.

Also, **Jeremiah 32:27** says that, behold, I am the LORD, the God of all flesh: is there anything too hard for me? We shall keep digging, for it is not over until the Lord says so. May our enemies locate us today as they located Isaac so they could make treaty in Jesus name! May favour locate us even as we reject lack and famine in our life and the assignment and weapons of the enemies for our life, in the name of Jesus Christ our Lord and Saviour.

Everything done against us to spoil our joy is destroyed in Yeshua (Jesus Christ) Mighty Name.

It does not matter whether we deserve it or not, but by faith we receive unquantifiable favour from the Lord like Isaac in Jesus name. Father God disgrace every power that is out to steal your program for our life in the name that is above all other names Yeshua Hamashiach (Jesus Christ). We read in the book of **Matthew 10:22-23** that, you will be hated by everyone because of me, but the one who stands firm to the end will be saved Halleluiah Amen.

Accordingly, **Philippians 1:29-30** say, for it has been granted to you on behalf of Christ not only to believe in him, but also to suffer for him, since you are going through the same struggle you saw I had, and now hear that I still have. Therefore, the reason why you and I should not be terrified is because to you that very thing was given graciously as a favour for the sake of Christ and on His behalf, not only to be believing on Him but also to be suffering for His sake and in and on His behalf. Know that, belief is enough to be assured of heaven, since we have been justified through faith, we have peace with God through our Lord and Saviour Yeshua Hamashiach (Jesus Christ the Messiah).

I mentioned about Elijah in chapter six brethren, and I cannot finish talking about Elijah and forget to mention Elisha. Elijah had a relationship with Elisha and Elisha had a relationship with Gehazi. Gehazi called him master, while Elisha called Elijah my Father and so he was blessed.

He followed his master and received what he desired as he walked with him. What have you desired in your walk with God today? He is the same yesterday to and forever. He is the one who was the one who is and the one who is to come. Elisha did not settle for nothing but kept pursuing his master until he saw him taken away by a whirl wind and got the mantle. Where have you settled?

We read in **Proverbs 27: 18-19**, that the one who guards a fig tree will eat its fruit, and whoever protects their master will be honoured. As water reflects the face, so one's life reflects the heart. This is to say, as in water face answers to face, as the image of a man's face in the water answers to his natural face who looks into it, so, one's life reflects the heart. Whoever tends a fig tree will eat its fruit, and he who guards his master will be honoured. As in water face reflects face, thus the heart of man reflects the man **(ES)**.

Accordingly, you can only receive from your father. He is your guide your instrumentalist in leading you. A father engages in deep conversation with his children, heart to heart conversation that impacts more than facts and teaches his children wisdom. Don't forget we are talking on where we are settled brethren. You need ask yourself as you continue to read this chapter and this book as a whole. Where do I want to settle?

In **Proverbs 23:22** we read, listen to your father, who gave your life, and do not despise your mother when she is old and also **Proverbs 23:24**. The father of a righteous child has great joy; a man who fathers a wise son rejoices in him.

Then in **Proverbs 20:7** we read, the righteous lead blameless lives; blessed are their children after them. Therefore, brethren It's not by power not by might. Who art thou mountain to stand before Zerubbabel as we read in **Zachariah 4:7**. Our strength can do very little but if we trust God, we shall be like mount Zion that cannot be shaken.

May I remind us at this time a man called Jehu had no track record and was able to destroy the whole house of Ahab for he was given the assignment to do so. You must then have good a track record beloved. Networking is key avoid just me, myself and I. No man is an island my reader. Get connected to others for two are better than one. For the bible says one can chase a thousand and two ten thousand. Desire also to have a father or an authority that can speak in your life and release a blessing.

The scriptures in **Proverb 4:7** we read, Wisdom is the principal thing; therefore, get wisdom, and with all thy getting get understanding. Wisdom comes from |God and the fear of God is the beginning of wisdom.

Learn to fear God with all your heart, soul and body. Wise and godly men, in every age of the world, and rank in society, agree that true wisdom consists in obedience, and is united to happiness.

Therefore, get wisdom, and no matter what it takes take pains for it. The bible has made us to know in **1 Corinthians1:27-29** that God said he uses the foolishness of this world to conform the wise and God chose the weak things of the world to shame the strong (mighty) so no man can boast.

In **Acts 20:10** Paul went down, threw himself on the young man and put his arms around him. "Don't be alarmed," he said. "He's alive!" Remember when Paul preached for too long and a man fell from third floor due to sleep and he died. He stretched on him, like Elijah and the dead boy came back to life. You cannot try it today in our modern world. Why? Fear because if you try it you may end in prison. What I am trying to say is from the upper room, where they were assembled, into the court, yard, or street, where he fell; or into the lower room of the house, where he was brought when taken up.

Eutychus, a young man fell asleep due to the long nature of the discourse Paul was giving, and so he fell from a window out of the three-story building, and died. Paul fell on him, and embracing him; praying over him, as Elijah and Elisha did, in the book of **1 Kings 17:21** which says, then he stretched himself out on the boy three times and cried out to the LORD, LORD my God, let this boy's life return to him and in **2 Kings 4:34**, then he got on the bed and lay on the boy, mouth to mouth, eyes to eyes, hands to hands. As he stretched himself out on him, the boy's body grew warm.

Likewise, Paul said trouble not yourselves, to the friends and relations of the young man and to the disciples present, who were concerned at this accident, both for the young man's sake, and lest it should be enhanced to the disadvantage of the Gospel by the enemies of it, for his life, being blamed upon the apostle's falling on him, and praying over him or he said this as being fully assured that it would return, in like manner as Christ said concerning Jairus's daughter, **Luke 8:52**, meanwhile, all the people were wailing and mourning for her. Stop wailing, Jesus said. She is not dead but asleep and **Luke 8:55** says, Her spirit returned, and at once she stood up. Then Jesus told them to give her something to eat.

Do not settle at where your problem has met you. Your enemy may be following you to destroy you using demonic surveillance but fear not. Arise and refuse to allow the spirit of intimidation to keep you down. The devil only comes to steal, to kill and to destroy but Jesus came so that we may have life and have it to the full. It could be sickness or death famine in thy land but arise and keep digging. Do not stop until you receive your breakthrough. It's not over until the Lord says it is over  Where have you settled my reader?

## CHAPTER ELEVEN

## DEALING WITH CULTURAL ISSUE IN A SECRET PLACE.

Unless we wait in our **secret place** this might be a hard topic to tackle, but I will lightly touch it until further recordings. We need to be true believers who are doers of the word and not only hearers. We must know the will of God for our lives. According to Jews you cannot ill-treat widows or orphans. Today many of us do not care for them. We actually manipulate them and even take what they have. Where have you settled even in your mind? Use the word of God to check if you are in the mind of God because the word is our mirror. Could you have lost your culture and you don't even remember the widows, the widowers and orphans?

In the book of **Deuteronomy 26:12** the bible says, When you have finished setting aside a tenth of all your produce in the third year, the year of the tithe, you shall give it to the Levite, the foreigner, the fatherless and the widow, so that they may eat in your towns and be satisfied.  Recollect I mentioned this in another way but Palestine widows and orphans were the two most vulnerable groups in ancient Israelite society, for they had no husband or father.  The biblical prophecy often stresses the need to protect them.

It is good to emphasises that there is need to care for orphans and widows in their affliction even as we settle. The bible records in the book of **James 1:27** that, Pure and genuine religion in the sight of God the Father means caring for orphans and widows in their distress and refusing to let the world corrupt you.  How then as believers do, we deal with the cultural matters that affect us in many ways of life? Are we able to take care of those needy in our community? Can we take care of divorced women, orphans, widows, widowers and even homeless people withing our vicinity?

Palestinian Hebrew women were among the poorest in the world in Jesus' day.  This was due in no small part to Roman agricultural practices that which divested the Israelites (particularly Galileans) the need of their ancestral lands and increasingly impoverished the population. Hebrew women were not allowed to divorce their husbands, but could be divorced for anything from burning the dinner (Hillel) to adultery (Shammai). In a culture in which women did not survive, unless they were linked to the patriarchal household, it was disastrous to be divorced.

What am saying to you my reader is that the scriptures say, Listen, my son, to your father's instruction and do not forsake your mother's teaching according to **Proverbs 1:8**. My son, keep your father's command and do not forsake your mother's teaching **Proverbs 6:20**. You are blessed beyond measure for the Lord is in need of you. So, cultures cannot deter God to bless you but follow the counsel of God through your leaders or authority.

You are the salt of your generation and so the Lord need to use you, be loosed in Jesus Name. Let's tell God to change our mind and give us new perspective as we become transformed to be like Him. The situations we had previously will change if we have the desire to change.

The book of **Isaiah 54:14 -17**, tells us that; in righteousness you will be established, Tyranny will be far from you; you will have nothing to fear.  Terror will be far removed; it will not come near you.  If anyone does attack you, it will not be my doing; whoever attacks you will surrender to you. "See, it is I who created the blacksmith who fans the coals into flame and forges a weapon fit for its work.  And it is I who have created the destroyer to wreak havoc.  Sometimes when God want us to listen to Him and we are not He causes havoc so we can be still and hear Him.

Therefore, God gives idea to perform but the promise is in verse 17 of **Isaiah 54**, which says that there is no weapon forged against you will prevail, and you will refute every tongue that accuses you.  For this is the heritage of the servants of the LORD, and this is their vindication from me, declares the LORD.  If you agree with the ideas to cause havocs then it will work but when you refuse to become the salt of your situation, environment and heal them from the source for you are the salt, the preservative then there will be consequences.

Remember the donkey had to agree for the master to use it for two cannot walk together unless they agree. Forget not that the owners had put limit on it just like some people have labelled us on our past. The donkey had a past, but the master wants it. He knew that it was the donkey which will do the triumphant entry to Jerusalem as it shows off the salt of the world. The donkey situation was changed. Whoever had put us in a cage it's too late for the salt of the world has come to lose us from all bondage. You and I must carry the Master and let the world see that he has made beauty out of ashes.

When you read **Luke 7:12,** it says honouring the dead was important in Jewish tradition and I wonder whether this is the scripture, chief mourners read, because hired mourners were hired to draw attention to the procession during the funeral narrated in this scripture. Mourning could have continued for 30 days and would have left this woman a beggar. God forbids. He is the God of the living as long as Jesus Christ came to set us free from cultures that has kept us bound by their tradition and believes. And So, every satanic embargo placed on God's people to influence and manipulates them to work contrary in their mind and not the will of God be destroyed in Jesus Mighty Name.

This year every dead situation must change in our life. It's not time to negotiate with the chief mourners for Jesus Christ has shown up in the procession. When Yeshua shows up in your situation even your enemies will confess that He is the Lord. Even when Lazarus a friend of Jesus died, he took long but He knew he is the life and the resurrection and he was going to revert that situation and glorify His father. So, every dead situation that has made many of our friends and enemies continue to help us mourn receive the resurrection of our Lord and Saviour.

We shall return the missiles to the sender as we enter into the New Year/season there shall be none of us who will die prematurely in Yeshua's Name. We are crossing to the other side and nothing can stop us not even death of our loved ones, not any kind of sickness and disease, not any storm can stop us to enter into our season of rest in Yeshua's Mighty Name. The Master is in the boat.

The storm is only to increase our faith because on the other side we shall find challenges and terminators waiting but do not be afraid, for the one who spoke into existence the lion of the tribe of Juda is on our side.

When he roars every other lion goes to hide because He is the lion of the tribe of Judah. There are people who may or can delay you from completing your assignments, because they have of a different opinion with you. Myself I call them HATERS OF PROGRESS. My brother, my sister let us avoid them and if possible, run away from their camp.

The bible tells us to flee from the devil and he will flee away from us. Do not worry He who began the good works in you will complete it in His Name and make it beautiful at his own appointed time. He is coming with a reward in His hands and if you do His will, He will never forget you. You can never be forgotten for He is a rewarder of those who diligently seek Him.

You must learn to wait and walk with God and to cultivate your salvation with fear and trembling. When you cultivate that relationship, by spending time in His Word, taking time for prayer, and taking every opportunity you can to be involved in church and also on small cell groups for bible study opportunities. When you seek these disciplines in your life, God will begin the first steps to revealing His plan to you.

The bible says, Trust in the Lord with all your heart, and lean not on your own understanding. In all your ways submit to Him, and He will make your paths straight according to **Proverbs 3:5-6**. My reader you are different from everyone else, not even your culture for you have the mark of our Lord Jesus Christ (Yeshua Hamashiach).

Also, surrendering your will to God. Obey what you already know to be His will for a big part of God is already delineated carefully through His word and we need to know obedience is an important aspect.

Seeking God input is important according to **proverbs 11:14** which says, for lack of guidance a nation falls, but victory is won through many advisers.

Getting involved with the community of believers makes it easier to discern the will of God for two are better than one. Just pay attention to the Holy Spirit and above all apply **1Peter 4:10** that, each of you should use whatever gift you have received to serve others, as faithful stewards of God's grace in its various forms.

Furthermore, **Psalms 37:4-5** tells us to take delight in the LORD, and he will give you the desires of your heart. Commit your way to the LORD; trust in him and he will do this. This passage teaches us that when we are walking with the Lord, He will actually let us do many things that we love, for when you are close to God, he shapes your desires so that you only desire what he has called you to do. His plan and will becomes a super exciting adventure.

## CHAPTER TWELVE

## HE MAKES EVERYTHING BEAUTIFUL (REVELATION 21:4).

As I conclude this book, let me take this opportunity to thank our heavenly father for the wonderful grace that we have been given free through Jesus Christ, for enabling us to reach this day that is very important in our church calendar. Let me wish you much blessings from the Lord and may you continue depending on Him. The Lord says in everything acknowledge Him and He will straighten your path. It is my prayer to encourage the church to continue trusting in the Lord always and lean not into our own understanding.

It is a great privilege to join other believers as we celebrate the fact that we are still holding on to our Lord and Saviour even at this time. I know that as long as the Lord is leading, His church will move to greater heights as we prepare in prayer for His second coming in Yeshua's Mighty Name.

This is a period of favour, and divine acceleration and supernatural transformation. You shall live to inspire every culture, family and individual to become more pleasing to the Lord. I believe it has been a long journey since the inception of the church but God has been faithful.

May God help His church to think big and shake off its former dust for the later shall be greater. God says, behold I am doing a new thing for He is the beginning and the end. Your faith has been built and founded through His church and my prayer is for God to give us more years so He can continue being manifested in people's lives as we wait patiently for Him to come and take us home.

When we study eschatology, we hear of Mary Agreda who was a catholic saint Born in Spain prophesied about Mary the mother of Christ and lived between 1602 B.C and 1666. She also prophesied and reported the victory of Christ over hell. She was sixteen years old when she met Mary the mother of Jesus. Very significant number.

The book of **Ecclesiastes 3:11** has assured us that God will and He has made everything beautiful in its time.  He has also set eternity in the human heart; yet no one can fathom what God has done from beginning to end.  This is to say, Beauty, though distinct from love, is the minister of love and its rays is edged and fringed with mercy.  It's every form bears the inscription, "God is love."  When it beams upon us from the heavens, it reveals His benignity (compassion, or kindness).  When it glows on the earth, or gleams from the ocean, it reflects His smile.

When it stretches its many coloured bow on the cloud or the water fall, it utters His thoughts of peace. Saints, when the Creator, formed the world, He had the **loveliness** of things before Him as an end and object, as well as the usefulness of things.  And so, wherever we walk, we see reflected love of beauty in the Divine mind.  And the more meticulously we examine the works of God, the more exquisite is their beauty.  God loves to have things beautiful: and it is wise for us to foster in ourselves the love of beauty.

Everything is beautiful in its appointed time. The fulness and harmony of things is largely an element of beauty. The order, the perfect sequence, of nature's law is as wonderful as the varied beauty of her forms. "Every winter turns to spring." In our years walking with God we may have seen all the storms but God has made everything beautiful at his appointed time. Storms, winter, spring autumn and summer has come and gone, but God who is so merciful has made us to remain.

No wonder **Psalm136:26** says, "O give thanks to the God of heaven, for his steadfast love endures forever." Let me say a good follower of our Savoir in the period we are in should be like Him the King of glory. For us to be an effective followers of Jesus Christ (Yeshua Hamashiach), a Navigator, a guiding force, a helper, a teacher, a prophet, a pillar of strength for everyone around, then we must have an ability to embrace and love all. We must be focused and passionate (Zealous), authentic and a Paul to Timothy to many as he focused to Jesus the only Superstar.

All this is measured not by what we give but by the spirit that you give it with.

Therefore, I encourages you not to settle in Moab even when those around you tell you that you cannot make it. Sometimes, we have no friends, they say to us, you are overweight even asking how can you carry heels like that with your body.  Refuse to be branded and you must pick yourselves up and follow Jesus to your next level of having an intimacy relationship with the Master.  Always remember you are beautiful, fearfully and wonderfully made with the image of God.  I pray that the light of God shines down upon His church, at this end time.  Even as we keep sanitizing our hearts with the blood of Jesus until we become that finished product He is looking for.

May the Lord continue to bless you my reader as I encourage and challenge you to appreciate the goodness of God in your lives and for his peace that reigns in the church and in our families in this dispensation.  We will keep pressing on and the Lord will reward us for He is the rewarder of those who diligently seek Him. We need to remember that the journey has just started and in our quest for better society the church must be visible. I pray for trace me anointing upon the church of God in Yeshua's Mighty Name. This can only be practical when you find yourself and avoid associating with people who do not know your worth, because they will help you to be put in the wrong place. Do not allow anyone to put you down for you are a child of God, who has a good plan for you.

What I can say at this juncture is every church, every family or individual has challenges but when we overcome them, we forget all the pain. Remember when you went to church and could be the doors were closed on you? You began to worship God anywhere maybe even under a tree. That enthusiasm to serve and praise God, never quench it. Thank God for the Christians who has continued to trust that God has truly called them to keep pushing on by faith until He comes.

God has helped you and you have survived the storms and you will keep jumping any handle that comes for no weapon formed or fashioned against the church shall prosper. Never allow fear and hurting for the mistake you did, to tell you that you cannot make ends meet. We must get out of that little voice and avoid staying in our old stage and get exposed to other areas which will expose us to what God want of every one of us.

Irrespective of the circumstances when Jesus shows up all what we desired will be satisfied and that is why **1Thessalonian 3:3-4** says that no one would be unsettled by the trials because we were destined for them. The Lord has surely come and wiped away our tears and shame. To God be all the glory. **2 John 1:8** tells us to take care that we do not loose what we have laboured for but that we will be rewarded fully. How does this happen, that after all the work one has done lose a reward? This can only happen through disobedient and pride which comes before fall. We will surely stand brethren in the power of His might. He has promised and He will see us through to our expected end.

In the book of **Romans 8:18** we hear, the bible says "I consider that our present sufferings are not worth comparing with the glory that will be revealed in us". Soon what we have laboured for will be brought to light and we enter into our rest if we faint not. God will make everything beautiful at His time.

The book of **Psalm 30** reads, "I will extol thee, O Lord, for thou hast drawn me up, and hast not let my foes rejoice over me. O Lord my God, I cried to thee for help, and thou hast healed me. O Lord, thou hast brought up my soul from Sheol, restored me to life from among those gone down to the Pit. Sing praises to the Lord, O you his saints, and give thanks to his holy name. For his anger is but for a moment, and his favour is for a lifetime for weeping may tarry for the night but joy comes with the morning.

As for me, I said in my prosperity, 'I shall never be moved.' By thy favour, O Lord, thou hardest established me as a strong mountain; thou didst hide thy face, I was dismayed. To thee, O Lord, I cried; and to the Lord I made supplication;

'What profit is there in my death, if I go down to the Pit? Will the dust praise thee? Will it tell of thy faithfulness? Hear, O Lord, and be gracious to me! O Lord, be thou my helper!' Thou hast turned for me my mourning into dancing; thou hast loosed my sackcloth and girded me with gladness, that my soul may praise thee and not be silent. After all this then we should sing the song of praise. His promises are yes and amen and since He has promised He will do.

The bible in the book of **Malachi 3:16-17** has made us to know that, those who fear the Lord talked with each other and the Lord listened and heard. And then a scroll of remembrance was written in his presence concerning those who feared the Lord and honoured His name. May you be remembered for honouring the Lord and especially in the years that we have all survived hidden under His canopy in Yeshua (Jesus Name).

THE MYSTERY WHICH REMAINS, AND WILL REMAIN is no man can find out. We do well to remember that what we see is only a very small part indeed of the whole.

Only a page of the great volume, only a scene in the great drama, only a field of the large landscape and we may well be silenced, if not convinced. But even that does not cover everything. We need to remember that we are human, and not divine; and that we, who are God's very little children, cannot hope to understand all that is in the mind of our heavenly Father. We cannot expect to fathom his holy purpose, to read his unfathomable thoughts.

We have seen enough of His divine wisdom, holiness, and love to believe that, when our understanding is enlarged and our vision cleared, we shall find that all the paths of the Lord were mercy and truth, even those which most troubled and bewildered us when we dwelt upon the earth. But one thing which is an assurance is when he shall appear, we shall be like him for we shall see him as he is.

The word of God says in **Deuteronomy. 8:7-18**, God was and is speaking that after we have come to a land full of bread and honey, when we eat, we should not forget his doings. He is the same yesterday today and forever.

He destroyed before, He can do it again and we should not forget. Let us fear Him who is Holy and faithful to the letter.

The book of **Job 36:11** Affirms, what Job said, if you obey and serve, then you will spend the rest of your days in prosperity and thy years in contentment. My reader, keep serving the Lord always for He who began the good works is faithful to complete it. May God locate us in the area of lack, sickness, singleness, stagnation and take us to greater heights in Jesus name. We must cross over to the other side. As we wait on the second coming of our soon coming King, may we remember to be focused to follow Him and Him alone who has given us Christ the hope of glory as our role model.

My reader, do not settle for less but keep digging and never settle before you get to your Rehoboth. The earth is the Lord's and the fulness thereof. May the Lord make your journey successful as you walk this walk with Him in Yeshua's Name for service in God is the pathway to greatness.

Saints of God all we need is in **John 6:29** believe in the one He has sent.  May the Lord help us so, we are able to say O Lord my God; I will give thanks to thee forever."

**Isaiah 6:1** says, finally; Isaiah spoke and said, the year that King Uzziah died, I saw the Lord seated on a throne, high and exalted, and the train of his robe filled the temple.  So, I said "Woe is me for I am undone! Because I am a man of unclean lips, and I dwell in the midst of a people of unclean lips; for my eyes have seen the King, the Lord of hosts."

Also, I heard the voice of the Lord, saying: Who shall I send, and who will go for us?" Then I said "Here am I! Send me." Isaiah emphatically (categorically) answered God's call just like we have and for the years we have been in God we have waited on God patiently and persistently.  May the Lord remove every evil from our face and help us to reflect His glory.

Possibly, the Lord will do great and mightier works through His temple which me and you are, such that we will be noticed for it will be too visible not to be noticed by Nations and among our people in Yeshua (Jesus Christ) Name. From now I say it again and again, do not trouble me for I have the mark of the Lord **Galatians 6:17**. I am marked for eternity and no devil can stop it because I believe, I have received by faith life eternal even as we open our eyes to His harvest field in Yeshua's Name.

The scriptures in **Psalms 92:12** tells us that, the righteous shall flourish like a palm tree; they will grow like a cedar of Lebanon, planted in the house of the Lord they will flourish in the courts of our God. They will still bear fruit in old age; they will stay fresh and green. May this season and the seasons to come, be a time of uplifting, double portion and covenant restoration in Yeshua's name. God has made and will make everything beautiful if we faint not.

In conclusion, brethren may **Psalms 103** be your song, my soul, give thanks to the Lord, all my being, bless His holy name. My soul, give thanks to the Lord and never forget all His blessings. It is He who forgives all your guilt, who heals every one of your ills, who redeems your life from the grave, who crowns you with love and compassion, who fills your life with good things, renewing your youth like an eagle's.

The Lord does deeds of justice, gives judgment for all who are oppressed. He made known His ways to Moses and His deeds to Israel's sons. The Lord is compassion and love, slow to anger and rich in mercy. His wrath will come to an end. He will not be angry forever. He does not treat us according to our sins, nor repay us according to our faults.

For as the heavens are high above the earth, so strong is His love for those who fear Him. As far as the east is from the west, so far does He remove our sins? As a father has compassion on his sons the Lord has pity on those who fear Him. For He knows of what we are made, He remembers that we are dust.

As for man, his days are like grass, he flowers like the flower of the field. The wind blows and he is gone and his place never sees him again. But the love of the Lord is everlasting upon those who hold Him in fear; His justice reaches out to children's children when they keep His covenant in truth, when they keep His will in their mind. The Lord has set His sway in heaven, and His kingdom is ruling over all.

Give thanks to the Lord, all His angels, mighty in power, fulfilling His word, who heeds the voice of His word. Give thanks to the Lord, all His hosts, His servants who do His will. Give thanks to the Lord, all His works, in every place where He rules. My soul, give thanks to the Lord.

I declare and decree we shall be restored of all the stolen glory, peace, favour, money, promotion and our prayer life in Yeshua's Mighty Name. Lord, we will sacrifice our life, for you Jesus, because, you did good things for us. Once again you did good things for us and so, we will sacrifice our life for you Jesus.

All I know is the miracle worker is on the way with our miracle and the life eternal which He promised and is undisputable.

In the book of **Proverbs 18:10** the bible says, the name of the LORD is a strong tower, the righteous run to it and they are safe. I declare you shall not end this journey empty handed in Yeshua's Name. My reader, you will receive that which God has promised you, if you faithfully hold onto the faith.

**Psalm 91: 1-2** postulates that, whoever dwells in the shelter of the Most- High, will rest in the shadow of the Almighty. I will say of the Lord, "He is my refuge and my fortress, my God, in whom I trust." My reader I beseeches you to hind in the pavilion of the King of kings and keep trusting God. I inspire you to pray again, as this book is talking so much about the **Secret Place**.as it's title. This is the place of your waiting on God and I hope you will be exited and your spirit lifted up to be able to go in your **secret place** before it's too late for God is making everything beautiful.

Please let's pray these prayers as you continue to read this book and waiting in your secret place to receive from the Lord.

## Prayer:

- I terminate any weapon of untimely death against my family, my church, and my children in Jesus name.
- Oh! God avenge for me, my church my family my children in Jesus name.
- I secure the harvest of the church, my family my children in Yeshua's Name.
- I declare new beginning and release divine provision for my church, my family, my children, my husband, my wife in Yeshua's Name.
- Oh Lord may my enemies and their stronghold be shattered to pieces by thunder of God in Yeshua's Name.
- Any evil charm or sacrifice buried because of me, the church, family, and children be exhumed by earthquake in Yeshua's Name.

- Every collective captivity receives fire and divine axe in Jesus name.

- I challenge by fire every throne challenging my enthronement through the bond of collective captivity, catch the fire of God in Yeshua's Name.

- Father God disgrace every power that is out to steal your program for my life in the name of Jesus Christ (Yeshua Hamashiach).

- Today we receive angelic transportation to where God wants us to be in Yeshua's Name.

- It does not matter whether I deserves it or not, I receives unquantifiable favour from the Lord like Isaac in Yeshua's Name.

- Let God who answers by fire spit fire into my situation today and wipe out failure and defeat in Yeshua's Name

- Let every spiritual cobweb spread over my documents be roasted by fire in Yeshua's Name

My reader, I encourages you to purchase your future blessings and security by positioning your faith to obedience in God and His word.

It's your time to come from the back to front by applying divine obedience to GOD and turn your story around. It's time to reprogram your mind, and time to reform your thinking for there is no other better time to embrace your new beginning. You will surely see the greatness of God.

May the blood of Jesus Christ be transfused into our blood system and we thank you Yeshua (Jesus the Christ) for spoiling principalities and powers, making a show over them openly, triumphing over them according to **Colossians 2:15**. We are more than a conqueror in Yeshua's Name.

Consequently, we need kindness and love to see and wait for the end of all the struggles. I trust this book has blessed you in Yeshua's Mighty Name. My reader, I speak the blessing of Abraham, Isaac and Jacob over your life my beloved of the Lord and according to **Numbers 6:24-25**,

May the Lord bless and keep you, may the Lord make his face shine on you and be gracious to you. May God be a canopy over you and may He hind you under His pavilion until we meet again. Shalom.

## Note that:

The bible says, and how from infancy you have known the Holy Scriptures, which are able to make you wise for salvation through faith in Christ Jesus **2Timothy 3:15**. Please if you would like to give your life to the Lord so that He can take charge over your life, please do so and pray the prayer below and you will become a new creation. "And you shall know the truth and the truth shall set you free" according to **John 8:32**.

## PRAYER OF REPENTANCE:

Lord Yeshua (Jesus the Christ) I repent of my sins and practices, I renounce my evil life of sin. Come into my life, forgive me, cleanse me receive me and write my name in your book of life.

I confess today you are my Lord and Saviour. Forgive my sins and delete my name from the book of destruction and write my name in the Lamb's book of life. Thank you for forgiving my sins and making me a new creature. Thank you, Lord, for saving me. I am saved by the blood of our Lord and Saviour. Help me to live my life for you in Jesus Mighty Name (Yeshua Hamassiach) I pray thee.

Amen!!!!

YOU CAN ALSO BUY THE FOLLOWING BOOKS FROM BISHOP DR. VANESSA IN AMAZON.UK

**Occupy till I come**

**The Greatness of God**

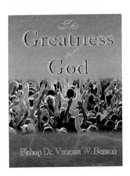

**The Power of Going Through**

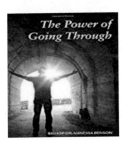

# THE SECRET PLACE

## UNLEASING GODS POWER

## DIVINE CONNECTION